LANDMARK V

T

Gambia

Andy Gravette

Published by
Landmark Publishing Ltd
Ashbourne Hall, Cokaye Ave, Ashbourne
Derbyshire DE6 1EJ England

As special correspondent for The Sunday Times, author Andy Gravette was based in Monrovia, West Africa, during the 1970s. On breaks from his work in Liberia, Andy would travel the short distance to The Gambia, to relax in this quiet backwater. Banjul, its capital, was still locally called Bathurst and, at that time, just a couple of hotels offered accommodation.

Prior to his death, Andy made numerous return trips to The Gambia, writing on a variety of local subjects which form the basis of this book. Andy's interest in wildlife and history led him to make frequent expeditions up-river, and across the border into Senegal.

Today the sun, sand and colourful culture are luring thousands of visitors to The Gambia's spectacular beaches and scenic countryside, which remain virtually unchanged.

This edition has been up-dated by Mustaph Choi (2002), now based in London, whose family still live in Gambia.

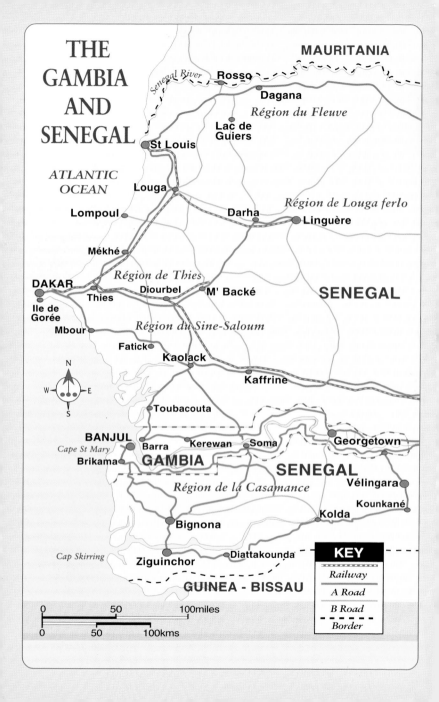

LANDMARK VISITORS GUIDE

The Gambia

Andy Gravette

Contents

Previous page: *A colourful craft market on Kotu Strand*

INTRODUCTION

J ust a short flight of five to six hours south from Europe brings the visitor into the exotic, colourful world of tropical West Africa. The Gambia, named after its wide river, is the nearest English-speaking African country to Britain and, immediately one lands at the small airport, the empathy with people of a common language but with an entirely different lifestyle is evident. A friendly, gregarious people with fascinating customs and culture, the Gambians are eager to please and to show visitors their exciting homeland.

The sights, sounds and smells of real Africa immediately endorse the fact that you have arrived in an unspoilt, charming country miles from the hubbub of the industrialised world. The sun's heat, bright voluminous costumes, exotic spices and fruits, all lure the traveller to explore this tiny

Above: A lazy day on the Atlantic coast at Kotu Beach

enclave further. Africa's smallest country is populated by around half a million inhabitants with wide-ranging roots. Most of the races of this part of the continent are represented here, from Moroccans to Mauritanians, making this country a melting pot of creeds and colours.

Take a trip to the location which spawned the novel *Roots*, a riverboat safari to birdwatch upstream and spot hippos and crocodiles, or mingle with a kaleidoscope of colourful traders in the local markets. The solemnity of the historic past, the sounds of African wildlife, and the great expanses of deserted beaches where local herdsmen bring their cattle to lick salt, all bring the pictures in holiday brochures to life. Traditional melodies and rituals from the heart of Africa, native dancing, drumming and tribal customs add to the experience of one of this continent's oldest countries.

As an extension to your visit to The Gambia, an excursion into French-speaking Senegal reveals a very different part of West Africa. With historic Dakar, Gorée and St. Louis, picturesque Casamance, Nio-kolo-Koba's teeming wildlife park and the fabulous bird life of the Saloum reserve, Senegal offers the visitor even more of an exotic African experience.

Climate & When to go

The Senegambia is in a sub-tropical zone and the hottest time of the year to visit is between the end of October and the beginning of May. This is the dry season and the hottest month is March. This makes it an ideal winter sunshine holiday. The month of April has the most sunshine hours during the day, with an average of 10 hours. The wet season runs from May to October and the coolest month is August.

From June to October, the humidity can be quite high, up to eighty per cent, and tropical rainstorms briefly punctuate the almost consistent sunshine. These need not deter the holi-day-maker, provided you have a light mac or umbrella during the rainy months. Typically tropical, torrential downpours can last several hours but clear suddenly when the hot sun dries the countryside remarkably quickly. August has the heaviest rainfall with up to 500mm. There is little or no rain during March and April.

Temperatures generally range from 30°C to 34°C, so there is little fluctuation, mean-ing that it is hot throughout the year. In the interior of Senegal, however, temperatures can

---

The Gambia and Senegal National Tourist Offices

The Gambia Tourism Authority (GTA)
The GTA was set up by an Act of Parliament in July 2001 as a public enterprise to develop, regulate and promote the tourism industry in The Gambia. It became operational in November 2001. *Address*: Gambia Tourism Authority, PO Box 4085, Bakau, The Gambia. ☎ (0220)462491 Fax (220) 462487. E-mail infor@gta.qm

UK office: The Gambia Tourism Authority, 57 Kensington Court, London, W8 5DG. ☎ (0207) 376 0093. Fax (0207) 937 9095.
E-mail office@ukgta.fsnet.co.uk

Senegal:
UK & Ireland, 11 Philimore Gardens, London W8 7QG, ☎ 0171 937 0925 Fax: 0171 937 8130
USA, 2112 Wyoming Ave. NW, Washington, DC 20008, ☎ 202 234 0540

be 3 to 5 degrees (C) higher. Near the coast a winter breeze cools the baking beaches. From January to April a dry, hot, Harmattan wind often blows off the Sahara desert bringing with it a fine, penetrating dust.

The Gambia and Senegal are attractive for sunseekers throughout the year although Europeans generally find that this destination is best for a winter holiday. Average maximum temperatures are shown right.

Getting there

A charter flight on a package deal is the easiest and least expensive way of getting to The Gambia and flights, six hours from London, are regular throughout the year. There are flights from America via Air Afrique to Dakar in Senegal and then on to The Gambia via Air Senegal. Yundum Airport in the Gambia is located in the centre of the Kombo Peninsula, a short coach ride from the main beach-side hotels and the capital, Banjul. Independent travellers might want to drive down through West Africa to The Gambia and will probably enter the country via the Senegambia Highway or along the Dakar-Banjul route.

(cont'd on page 12)

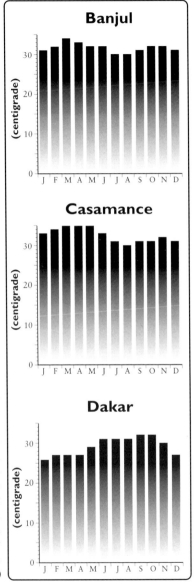

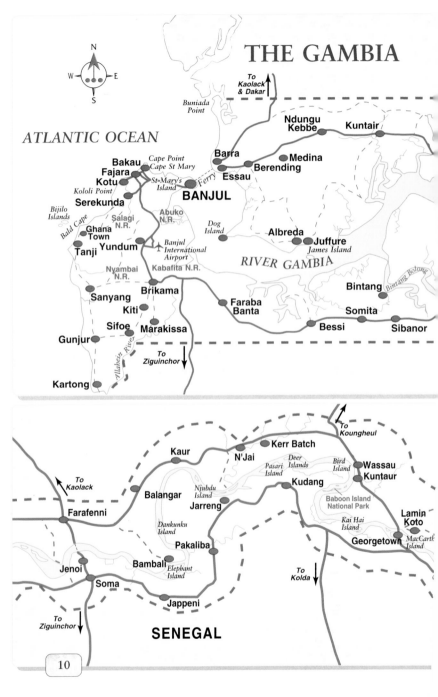

THE GAMBIA

N
W — E
S

Buniada Point

ATLANTIC OCEAN

To Kaolack & Dakar

Ndungu Kebbe
Kuntair

Bakau
Cape Point
Cape St Mary
Fajara
Kotu
St=Mary's Island
Kololi Point
Serekunda

Barra
Medina
Berending
Essau

BANJUL

Ferry

Bijilo Islands
Bald Cape
Salagi N.R.
Abuko N.R.

Dog Island
Albreda
Juffure
James Island

Ghana Town
Tanji
Yundum
Banjul International Airport
Kabafita N.R.

RIVER GAMBIA

Nyambai N.R.

Bintang
Bintang Bolong

Sanyang
Kiti
Brikama

Faraba Banta

Somita

Gunjur
Sifoe
Marakissa

Bessi
Sibanor

Allahein River

To Ziguinchor

Kartong

To Koungheul

Kaur
N'Jai
Kerr Batch
Deer Islands
Bird Island
Wassau
Kuntaur

To Kaolack

Balangar
Njubdu Island
Pasari Island
Kudang

Farafenni
Jarreng
Baboon Island National Park
Lamin Koto

Dankunku Island
Kai Hai Island

Pakaliba
Georgetown
MacCarth Island

Jenoi
Bambali
Elephant Island

To Kolda

Soma
Jappeni

To Ziguinchor

SENEGAL

10

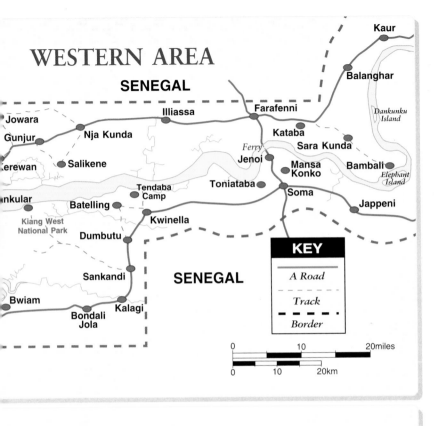

WESTERN AREA

SENEGAL

Kaur

Balanghar

Jowara

Gunjur

Nja Kunda

Illiassa

Farafenni

Dankunku
Island

Kataba

Sara Kunda

erewan

Salikene

Ferry

Jenoi

Mansa
Konko

Bambali

Elephant
Island

nkular

Tendaba
Camp

Toniataba

Soma

Jappeni

Batelling

Kiang West
National Park

Kwinella

Dumbutu

Sankandi

SENEGAL

KEY

A Road

Bwiam

Bondali
Jola

Kalagi

Track

Border

| 0 | 10 | 20miles |
| 0 | 10 | 20km |

THE GAMBIA EASTERN AREA

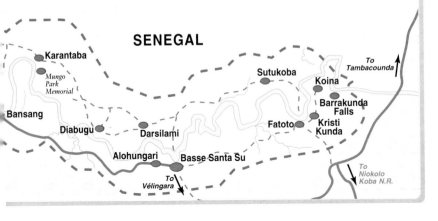

SENEGAL

Karantaba

Mungo
Park
Memorial

Sutukoba

Koina

To
Tambacounda

Barrakunda
Falls

Bansang

Diabugu

Darsilami

Fatoto

Kristi
Kunda

Alohungari

Basse Santa Su

To
Vélingara

To
Niokolo
Koba N.R.

Few passenger ships visit The Gambia but many stop over in Dakar.

Passports and jabs

A full valid passport is needed for anyone entering either Senegal or The Gambia.

Citizens of the United Kingdom, the Commonwealth, the Economic Community of West African States (ECOWAS) and other nations with a reciprocal visa abolition agreement with The Gambia do not require a visa to enter the country on holiday or on a business trip. All other nationalities should possess a visa, which is available from any of the Gambian embassies and consulates abroad: London, Paris, Washington, Brussels, Taipei, Rabat, Jeddah, Havana, Dakar, Lagos, Freetown and Bissau.

However, tourists and others travelling at the last minute will be allowed entry but will be required to submit their passport to the Department of Immigration in Banjul within 48 hours to be issued with a proper visa.

To visit Senegal, a visa should be obtained before travelling, unless one has a French, German, Italian, Moroccan, Tunisian or Algerian passport, or one from any of the country's neighbouring African States.

A **yellow fever** vaccination certificate may be required from travellers coming from endemic areas. Following WHO guidelines issued in 1973, a cholera vaccination certificate is not a condition of entry to Senegal. However, cholera is a risk in this country and precautions are essential. Up-to-date advice should be sought before deciding whether these precautions should include vaccination, as medical opinion is divided over its effectiveness. In Dakar doctors are plentiful and most medicines are available. Up-country however, facilities are minimal. For more information please contact the Senegalese Embassy: 39 Marloes Road, London, W8 6LA. ☎ (0207) 938 4048.

An international certificate of vaccination is no longer compulsory for visitors to the Gambia. However, a **yellow fever** vaccination will be required for travellers arriving from infected or endemic countries. It is not required for visitors from Europe and North America. The last yellow fever in The Gambia was in 1978 and there is no immediate danger to visitors. **Anti-malarial medicine** is however recommended and visitors should consult their doctors three weeks before travelling.

Aids is also prevalent in this part of Africa and sensible

precautions should be taken. In case of an emergency, most chemists stock an emergency medical pack which includes plasma and sterilised needles. It might be advisable to carry one of these packs at all times. A full insurance policy should be taken out before travelling.

Things to pack

Basic things to remember include a shawl or wrap for ladies and a jacket for men as the evenings can be cool, and a hat to protect from the hot sun during the day. Depending on when one is travelling, a folding umbrella might be considered. A waist-bag in which to keep valuables and essentials is a useful item, as is a money belt.

Sun creams and a mosquito repellent or device are almost essential. A small torch can be useful, as can a tin or bottle-opener. Take binoculars and camera, with spare batteries and sufficient film.

Small gifts for local children are always useful like ballpoint pens, pencils, sweets etc. Also, reading matter is in great demand and a few paperback books or magazines are eagerly received.

Food and drink

Few of today's Portuguese people realise that their forebears influenced the diet of the Senegambians. In the 16th century Portuguese traders, not only shipped great numbers of slaves from this coast to Brazil, but also brought back ground-nuts, manioc, cassava and maize from the New World. Settlers taught the Africans to cultivate these crops which now constitute part of the local staple diet.

Millet and sorghum are the mainstays of the dryer parts of Senegambia, and rice is grown in the wetter regions. In the northern part of Senegal, there is a distinct North African influence in their cookery, where couscous is made with millet instead of wheat. Groundnut paste and palm oil are used universally in Senegambian cookery. A great variety of vegetables, peppers and spices is grown throughout the region and mashed cassava, known as *fou-fou*, is a favourite ingredient of many main dishes.

The Senegalese menu is more cosmopolitan than that of The Gambia as their cookery has assimilated tastes from the French, Arabs, Portuguese and other African nations. However, because of the maritime location of both countries and their two respective large rivers, fish and shellfish are the main source of protein. Stews are popular and a visit to the local market where women prepare cauldrons of a wide selection of local dishes is a culinary revelation, especially if you sample a few.

Most hotels provide both local and European food and there is the opportunity to try more exotic foods like Lebanese, Chinese, Malaysian or Vietnamese. Several hotels tend to cater for the tastes of their most regular European visitors serving Scandinavian, German or French dishes. Naturally Senegal's hotel menus are distinctly French influenced.

Remember that Senegambia is predominantly Islamic and strict Muslims do not drink alcohol. However, there are no restrictions on its sale and the most popular drinks are the local beers, Julbrew in The Gambia and Flag in Senegal. Both are light, lager-like beers. Imported drinks are more expensive. Generally the tap water is safe to drink, but many visitors prefer bottled water, although this can be quite expensive. **Travellers in the interior should make sure they have sufficient water and should take water-purifying tablets or make sure water from wells is boiled and filtered.** Fruit should be peeled and some visitors might consider avoiding salads and other unwashed foods, including ice made from local water.

A short history

Senegambia and the Ancients

It is thought that the Senegambia region was the first part of West Africa to be settled by early nomadic tribes. Some experts date the first human occupation of the area back to 13,000 BC.

For centuries before the arrival of Europeans, the Gambia and Senegal rivers had been important trading routes. The Carthaginian ex-plorer, Hanno, made a journey to West Africa in 470 BC and wrote about elephants and hippopotami and the two rivers, Chertes in The Senegal, and Bambotu, in The Gambia. The Greek, Herodotus, visited the Senegambian coast in 445 BC and Polyibus, another Greek explorer visited the region in 146 BC. The ancients first indicated the existence of the West African coastline in a map of 141 AD and by 150 AD, Ptolemy was able to draw a passable indication of the routes of both the Senegal and Gambia Rivers. By this time a permanent settlement had been established by an indigenous civilisation at

Half a calabash shell serves as an excellent bowl in which to carry one's lunch to work.

The Brazilian Link

In the early 1500s, the Portuguese sailed the known seas, linking the New World – South America – with Europe. They brought commercially viable agricultural produce from Brazil to West Africa, in return for exporting slaves to their new colonies. The Canary Islands, an ideal location for passenger ships to stop over on their way to the southern parts of the New World, later became the mid-way point for trans-Atlantic crossings, using the favourable currents. Las Palmas was later superseded by the westernmost points that were then occupied on the African continent, St Louis, Senegal and James Island in The Gambia.

Just a decade or so ago, Concorde overflew the Senegambian coast. Probably unbeknown to the pilots, around fifty years previously, using St Louis in Senegal as a re-fuelling stage, an adventurous French aviator named Jean Mermoz first flew from Paris to Recife in Brazil. As this part of West Africa lies exactly halfway between France and Brazil, Aeropostal, the fore-runner of the French national airline service, ran a regular trans-Atlantic mail service between the three continents. This is what prompted the German airline, Lufthansa, to begin flights on their Dornier flying boats via Gambia to South America in 1932. Two years later, the first Zeppelin stopped here en-route to South America in 1934.

The British, during World War II, stopped the German service and its war-time activities, by stationing 20 Sunderland flying boats in The Gambia, having commenced a regular route from Banjul to Brazil in the late 1930s.

In 1959 the importance of Yundum became obvious to the Americans, who now use a base near the airport for monitoring their NASA satellite programmes, less than a quarter of a century after President Franklin D Roosevelt flew into the airport on his way to Brazil in 1944. Now the region is still one of the most important links between Europe and South America.

Jenne-Jeno in the south-east of the Senegambian region.

After this initial excursion by the ancients into the 'Dark Continent', the Sarahuley tribe had taken control of the entire region by the 5th century AD. They held sway in the Sene-gambia until the 8th century and slave, salt, iron and gold trading routes opened up large areas of West Africa. During the 9th century, the powerful Empire of Ghana (not to be confused with the more southerly country known as Ghana) had established itself inland from the coast.

For the following five centuries the Almoravids or Berbers from Mauritania, to the north of Senegal, dominated the northern part of the region.

As early as 1067 the Arab chronicler, El-Bakri, made note of the ancient tribal capital of the Ghana Empire which he named Cantor. Eventually the Mandingo and Susus tribes came down from the Futa Jallon heights, located at the source of the Gambia River, to control the Gambian river basin, leaving the Islamic tribes ruling most of what is today's Senegal.

Further tribal migration to the two rivers, prompted by severe droughts, resulted in the Wolof tribe settling on the north bank of the Gambia River and the Jolas on the south. However, the entire Gambia basin still remained part of the gold-rich Ghana Empire. By this time, Islam had swept down from the north in the wake of Arab missionaries to embrace most of the northern part of the Senegambian region. The Ghana Empire lasted until 1076 when it was defeated by the Almoravids under Abu Bakr. The great Mali Empire took control of the interior and remained in power during the 13th and 14th centuries.

Early explorers (1300-1560)

The first real map showing European knowledge of the Gambia and Senegal Rivers was produced by the French carto-grapher, Abraham de Cresques.

His impressions were soon superseded by the so-called Hereford Chart of 1307.

The first recorded expedition to the area was by another Frenchman, Dieppois, who claimed to have reached Gorée Island in Senegal in the early 15th century. At the same time, following the demise of the huge Mali Empire, the Fula tribes arrived in the Gambia region. Following the famous expeditions of Prince Henry of Portugal, Nuno Tristao reached the mouth of the Senegal River in 1443, venturing inland and further along the coast three years later. The Senegal River was then explored by another Portuguese, Dianaz Diaz, on behalf of Prince Henry, in 1444.

The Mande tribes in the south of Senegambia fought the predominantly Islamic tribes in the north between 1464 and 1493 until the incursion of the Europeans diverted the atten-tions of both towards a common foe. In 1455, Portuguese traders and explorers mapped a large part of the Gambia River. It was the Portuguese who introduced groundnuts and cotton into Senegambia and began the first European trade in the region. By 1510 the River Gambia had

(cont'd on page 20)

17

Checking out the birdlife

If you thought that birdwatching was strictly for the birds, you will think again when you arrive in The Gambia. Many visitors who previously could barely distinguish between a duck and a goose, have returned from holidaying in The Gambia with a new hobby – ornithology!

This may be Africa, the land of herds of wildebeest and thundering elephants, but unless you visit parts of Senegal, you will probably not see many of this continents's larger animals. However, The Gambia's stunning birdlife more than makes up for its lack of big game.

Within a few hours of landing, you won't be able to miss some of the country's more exotic birdlife. The first morning, you might be woken by the call of the bulbul which, together with red-billed hornbills, snowy-white egrets and fire-finches, will have made your hotel's gardens their home. Even on the beach, you cannot help but notice the comical antics of waders like the curved-billed sandpiper, the pied oyster-catchers and turnstones. A pirogue excursion on the wide river estuary brings the visitor into the domain of pelicans and cormorants, disturbing flocks of wildfowl nesting on the shoreline.

The more adventurous traveller might take a river boat trip, where bird-spotting quickly becomes contagious. Families of herons perch on the bankside mangroves and the cone-headed hammerkop vies with brightly-coloured kingfishers for the best perches on tree roots. Wheeling above, vultures are a common sight, and the occasional osprey or eagle is an added bonus. Soon you will be able to identify the awkward stance of the marabou stork, the nests of the weaver birds slung like discarded stockings from the branches of thorn bushes, and the brilliant plumage of rollers, sunbirds and parakeets.

There is little doubt that, by the end of your visit, the spectacular birds of The Gambia will have you hooked!

Opposite, clockwise from top left: Pink-backed or grey pelican, hadada ibis, curlew, red-billed hornbill, cattle egret, village weaver

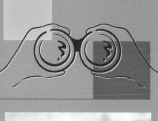

Origin of a name

The chronicler Ca'da Mosto noted the presence of exotic animals and golden jewellery in the region. He also noted the Arab caravans which traded in Negro slaves and, in 1465, he made further expeditions up the Gambia River in an attempt to barter with the local tribes. It is possible that the name 'Gambia' comes from the Portuguese word for exchange cambio.

appeared in its present name on the famous Lennox Globe and in the same year, the first consignment of slaves sailed for Europe from the Senegal.

The Portuguese had quickly adopted the Arab business of slavery, encouraged by Wolof chiefs who regularly raided weaker tribes to procure slaves. Loaisa, the notable Portuguese explorer, who had already charted part of the West African coast, made his celebrated 1525 voyage to Brazil. In subsequent years, the settlement of Brazil by the Portuguese would lead to the first stages of exporting slaves from Senegambia to the Americas. In all, over the next two hundred years, three million

Senegambians would be shipped to the Portuguese colony. The British were quick to follow in the footsteps of the Portuguese.

Slaves and settlers (1560-1660)

In 1562 the Elizabethan British began exporting slaves from the Gambian coast to the new sugar plantations of the West Indies. In 1570 the French also commenced trading for gold and slaves. However, the area remained undeveloped until the British settled on St. Mary's Island, using it as a trading post from 1587. In 1588, Antonio, Prior of Crato, won exclusive rights from Queen Elizabeth I of England to trade throughout the Senegambia region. The Dutch West Indies Company began trading from Gorée Island in 1617.

As early as 1621 the French had established a settlement at St. Louis in Senegal. They built a fortress and a slave trading station nearby, as the demand for slaves in their West Indian properties increased. Cardinal Richelieu commissioned the Senegal Company in 1633 and the Portuguese established a trading post on the Gambia River's south bank.

Around this time competition between the Dutch, French, Portuguese and British began to flare up. The German Duke of Courland set up a fort on the Ilha

Up-river exploration

An intrepid explorer named George Thompson charted the Gambia riverbanks as far up as Tendaba in 1619. Between 1620 and 1624, a Richard Jackson penetrated the country far up-river in search of legendary riches said to be located at the source of the Gambia.

de San Andre in the Gambia River in 1651. Prince Rupert was spurred to investigate tales of the West African 'El Dorado' by sailing down the Senegambia coast in search of the fabled city in 1652. The Swedes ousted the Dutch from Gorée Island in Senegal in 1655. They lost it back to the French under Admiral d'Estrees 22 years later.

Back on Ilha de San Andre in the middle of the Gambia River, the Duke of Courland, after nine years operating a slave trading station from his fort, lost the island to French privateers, only to reclaim it in 1660. In 1661 the English took the island from the Baltic Germans, naming it James Island after the heir to the English throne. James Island still stands in the river's estuary, 30 kms (19 miles) from the sea. It became an important slave-trading station and a collection point for slaves before they were shipped to the Americas by the British.

Skirmishes and colonisation (1660-1800)

So important to the slave trade was the strategic fort on James Island, that after severe bombardment, the Dutch ousted the English in 1662. The English resorted to fortifying a nearby island, Dog Isle, named after the barking baboons which were found there. The French also established a fortified outpost on the north side of the Gambia estuary, naming it Albreda. They were to hold this fort from 1670 for almost 175 years. Meanwhile, in 1680, in nearby Juffure, another trading station later to become famous in Alex Haley's novel *Roots*, was established by the English. Trade was so brisk that it led to the founding of the British Royal African Company in 1684.

There were now around ten slave stations operating along the Senegambian coastline and up the two major rivers. The French proceeded to take British-held Fort James, as James Island became known, in 1695, and the English returned to claim it in 1713. Six years later the renowned Welsh privateer, Hywel Davis, ransacked the fort. Another six years passed before an explosion in the fort's powder magazine, in 1725, blew the slave station to pieces. Although the fort and trade station was rebuilt the following year, by 1775 it was abandoned.

In 1765 The Gambia became a British Colony under rule from St. Louis in Senegal. This became the Crown Colony of Senegambia in 1768. By 1783, the French had driven the British onto the south side of the Gambia River but after the Treaty of Paris they retreated into Senegal.

Whilst the Europeans squabbled over trading rights and fought over strategic outposts, the indigenous population, a mixture of animists and Muslims, planned uprisings against the foreign insurgents. Marabouts, the native Islamic religious leaders, stirred up indigenous tribes against colonialism both in Senegal and in The Gambia. Frequent skirmishes between the Islamic tribes and European settlers began in 1798 and were to last for almost 90 years. French emancipation was first introduced towards the end of the 18th century, but the French slave trade was reinstated in 1802, continuing until 1848 on the orders of Napoleon.

Territorial divides (1800-1900)

Once Britain had abolished slavery in 1807, the Royal Navy established Bathurst (now Banjul) as a port from which to stem the illegal slave trade. Over the next few years they captured more than 100 slave ships off the Gambian coast. In 1816 Captain Alexander Grant negotiated with the Chief of Kombo for land on St Mary's Island, upon which Banjul was to be built.

From 1821 The Gambia was controlled by the British settlement of Freetown in Sierra Leone, to the south. The settlement of Bathurst grew up from 1828, two years after the construction of Fort Bullen on Barra Point opposite. Also in 1828, Grant acquired MacCarthy Island, 320 kms (200 miles) up the Gambia River, renaming the small settlement Georgetown.

In Senegal, many Africans were readily accepted into the French settlers' way of life. So much so that, from 1848, an African delegation from Senegal sat in the French parliament. Louis-Leon-Cesar Faidherbe

Above: *Waiting for the day's catch to come in*

Right: *Traditional fishing pirogues are hand-carved*

Below: *Cane-work stalls can be found in any market. Baskets make useful momentoes*

Early farming

Faidherbe was also responsible for the introduction of organised agriculture in Senegal, which up until his time had been largely unsuccessful. Extensive planting of groundnuts by local farmers eventually led to the country achieving a certain amount of self-sufficiency.

became the French Governor in 1854, basing himself in the main settlement, St. Louis.

He soon pushed the French boundaries southwards into Islamic territory, founding Dakar, the capital, in 1857 and withdrawing the French entirely from The Gambia. Faidherbe's forces pushed deeper into the Senegal interior, then the largest colony in Africa. He built numerous forts far up the Senegal River in order to quell tribal insurrection. The most notable Islamic African leader of this time, and a fearsome foe, was Lat Dyor, a chieftain whom eventually Faidherbe persuaded to fight on his behalf.

A rail system linking many major settlements in Senegal was heralded by the building of the Dakar to St. Louis line by 1886.

A degree of French citizenship was conferred on all Africans living in Senegal's major towns in 1887 and Dakar became the capital in 1902.

Towards independence

The Gambia was finally established as British in 1888 but it was still administered from nearby Sierra Leone. Bathurst officially became The Gambia's capital in 1892, but the land up-river did not become a protectorate until 1894.

By 1900 the boundaries of French Senegal had been established. This included the area south of The Gambia known as Casamance, which, until 1889, had belonged to Portugal. The first West African political party was established in Senegal in 1914 and, during World War II, Senegalese troops fought alongside the French. Gambians too, joined British ranks, serving mainly in Burma. Just after the war, in 1946, French citizenship was con-ferred on all the French West African states and Leopold Senghor represented Senegal in the French National Assembly. In 1960 Senegal became independent as part of the Mali Federation with Senghor as its first President. In 1980, Senghor stepped down in favour of his Prime Minister, Abdou Diouf.

Cannonball diplomacy

During the 1890s the French and English came to an agreement as to how they would divide up the land. It was decided that the British should fire their most powerful cannon from the centre of the Gambia River, James Island, into the north bank. Whatever distance the cannonball travelled would determine the extent of British territories each side of the river. It is commonly thought that the shot was fired north, landing in a place known as Berending, around 16 kms (ten miles) inland. This established the width of the British Protectorate at around twenty miles across. This boundary has changed over subsequent years, but still the story is relevant.

The Gambia, however, did not become independent until 1965, when it became an independent sovereign state with Dawda Jawara as its Prime Minister. Jawara was knighted in 1966 and, with the advent of the status of Republic in 1970, became the country's President. An uprising in The Gambia in 1981 prompted the intervention of Senegalese troops under the short-lived Confederation of Senegambia and, in 1994, after 29 years in office, Sir Dawda Jarawa was deposed. Captain Yayah Jammeh has been the elected Gambian Head of State since 1996.

1 WELCOME TO THE GAMBIA

A geographical outline

The Republic of The Gambia lies midway between the Tropic of Cancer and the Equator. It occupies a thin, flat strip of land on the West African coast, each side of the River Gambia, one of the continent's major waterways. The country is around 470kms (294 miles) from west to east. With an area of just over 11,000km² (4,300 sq miles), the parts of the country which do not border the river are arid and sandy.

The Atlantic Ocean coastline is just 80kms (50 miles) long, which includes the mile-wide mouth of the Gambia River estuary and 40kms (25 miles) of palm-fringed sandy beach. Just east of the tidal estuary, the river widens to 11kms (7 miles). Up-river, the long, narrow

Above: *West Africa's precious woods are used to carve imaginative sculptures*

country funnels to just 24kms (15 miles) wide. The Gambia River has no bridge and is navigable up to 200kms (125 miles) inland, being The Gambia's main arterial route. The French-speaking country of Senegal surrounds this tiny enclave on all sides apart from the country's short coastline and river estuary. The Gambia is on the same longitude as the Canary Islands and is on Greenwich Mean Time.

The people

The country has a population of approximately 1.4 million people (2001). Despite its small population it is a country of great diversity. There are nine ethnic groups comprising Wolof, Mandinka, Fula, Jolas, Sarahuleh creoles or AKU, Manjago, Bambara and others. The country is also home to large communities of other Africans particularly Senegalese. Some Lebanese businessmen and women and other European expatriates account for one percent of the population. More than 63 per cent live in the Gambia rural areas and are engaged in agriculture as the main source of income and sustenance.

The Gambia is the oldest English-speaking country in Africa and a few Gambians speak one or two other European languages. Many speak French due to the heavy influence from the surrounding country of Senegal. Polite and helpful, the Gambians are anxious to learn about the outside world, where you live, details of your family and what foreign countries are like. They may reciprocate by inviting you to experience their own lifestyle, even to visit their homes.

It is not without good reason that The Gambia is known as the 'smiling coast'. Gambians are naturally hospitable, to some visitors overtly so. You need a sense of humour and a receptive nature to appreciate the generosity of these people who are, in the main, genuinely interested in communicating with foreign visitors.

The **Muslim religion** makes for a rather macho society where the women's place is in the fields and at the hearth. However, just a visit to the local markets reveals that the large, bustling madams rule the roost amongst the traders' stalls. A woman travelling alone might experience the odd, half-hearted proposition which is a

27

Kola nuts

When travelling around The Gambia, and visiting local villages, it is a long-standing tradition to offer a small present to the village elder, or householder. In West Africa, the custom is to offer a few kola nuts, and it may be a good idea to carry some of these with you.

Kola nuts come from the kola tree which is a native of the region and is cultivated because the chestnut-size nuts, which grow in large pods, are highly prized. The nut is very bitter, but Africans derive great pleasure from chewing the nut as it contains a stimulant drug, a mild hallucino-genic and appetite and thirst-suppressant. Long distance drivers chew on the nuts to keep awake, and they are said to be the secret ingredient of Cola. The nuts come in varying colours, dark red, pink and the better, white variety. Buy only those which are white, hard and fresh.

way of life in The Gambia and is easy to decline politely.

The majority of Gambians are well-mannered and polite but some persistent pestering by itinerant traders, especially on the beaches, can be irritating to some visitors. A simple refusal without over-reaction is the best way to decline what is on offer. However, some approaches are purely innocent and intended just as a way of striking up a friendship with someone from a completely different world and way of life.

The people of The Gambia go about life in an unhurried and laid-back way which can seem alien and irksome to some visitors until one acclimatises to the *mañana* attitude. Strict Muslims do not drink alcohol or gamble and nudity is forbidden. However topless sunbathing in hotels or on the beach does not generally offend.

Arts and culture

The Gambians are natural artisans, adept at carving, straw and wickerwork, leatherwork, jewellery and textile work. There are craft markets in Banjul itself, but African-style market stalls are located near many hotels. These are known as *Bengdula*, the Mandingo word for meeting place. Polished hardwood carvings of African masks, animals, birds, people, bowls or ashtrays make excellent purchases. Gold and silver filigree necklaces, brooches, bangles and rings are classic examples of the Gambian craftmanship.

A popular local garment is known as the **Gambishirt**, a colourful, loose, embroidered garment crafted in the traditional style. Leatherwork and brilliantly-designed batikwork make good souvenirs. Batik can be bought as lengths of cloth or made up into any item you request. The Gambians are meticulous tailors who can produce suits, shirts etc by copying a pattern of whatever you want. *Lagos* is an indigo-dyed dark-blue to purple local cloth, popular with the Gambians themselves, which is printed in the area.

The Gambia is also the seat of many ancient and **traditional rituals** and customs involving intricate dancing and musical accompaniment (see below). The first unusual local instrument which the visitor will notice is the *kora*, a twelve-stringed harp-like lute. Other instruments of the Gambian 'orchestra' include the *rita*, a form of violin, the *balafon*, the *xalam* and *balonbota*, both basic forms of a banjo crossed with a

Musical instruments

Traditional West African dances of the region, like the 'devil dance', the 'leopard dance' and the silt dances, are often accompanied by local musicians playing a variety of traditional instruments. Apart from the vast ensemble of drums, from the *bata* to the *tamba* and the *djembes* to the talking drum, the *kora* is a favourite local stringed instrument. Built like a large lute, but with the strings of a harp, half a large gourd forms the soundbox from which projects a long, thin rosewood neck. The soundbox is covered in cow hide and a support for the 21 strings projects from the centre of this. The strings are plucked with the thumb and forefinger.

A percussion instrument like a huge, primitive xylophone, is the *balafon*. The 16 or so hardwood keys are mounted on a wooden frame and small gourds of varying sizes are suspended under them. The keys are struck with two sticks producing an almost metallic sound. The *shake-shake* is a hand-size gourd, rather like a *maraca*, but enclosed in a net from which beads, shells or buttons are suspended. *Claves* are two hardwood sticks, clapped together to create a rhythm.

guitar, and the *tama* a double-ended drum. Large calabashes, reed pipes, 'talking' drums and all manner of ingenious percussion instruments add to the distinctive Gambian sound.

Most Gambian dances are based on scenarios from everyday life, hunting, fishing, fieldwork etc and follow stories which can involve a wedding, circumcision, child-naming, or the welcoming of a guest. Local mythology also finds its way into the music and dance of The Gambia, where inanimate objects come to life, or animals develop a personality. Typical Mandingo dances which reflect everyday life are the *Sewruba* and the *Kankurang*; more wild and exciting is the dance known as the *Boocaraboo*.

One of The Gambia's best-known troupes is the Damel, who specialise in the energetic *Dagga* dance. Organised tourist shows not only include some spectacular local dancing and tribal music, but include traditional acrobatics known as masks, a word coming from masquerade, which is usually a tableaux of the interaction between the Africans and the gods of fire, wind, thunder, trees etc.

Feast days fall on the Muslim festivals of *Koriteh* and *Tobaski*, and Christmas is celebrated with processions of *fanals* or raffia and paper boats carried through the streets by small boys, celebrating the importance of the country's fishing industry.

Around 90 per cent of the population are Muslim, the rest follow the Christian and animist beliefs. However, a certain amount of pagan influence has survived to this day, even

Mosques

Throughout Islamic Gambia and Senegal you will see mosques of all shapes and sizes; from the region's tallest, the Great Mosque in Touba, Senegal, with its minaret towering 87m (286ft) into the desert sky, to the tiny clifftop shrine of Folonko in The Gambia. However, all mosques, whatever their size, have similar designs. The crescent moon, symbol of the Muslim religion, adorns the highest point. A place is designated for washing before prayer, and inside, the *mithrab* or prayer niche faces Mecca in Saudi Arabia, the Islamic holy city. If invited into a mosque, visitors should be appropriately covered and should remove their shoes.

Clockwise from top left:

a) Gambia's tie-dye artists create spectacular cloth designs;

b) a set of these Jola drums are called a 'bugarabu'

c) Serahuli woman wearing tribal, half-moon shaped gold earings;

d) traditional dance troupe;

e) many wood carvings follow centuries old designs;

mingled with Islam in a process called Syncretism. This mixture of beliefs involves the amalgam of pagan gods like Guruhi, god of thunder, Sene, god of rain, and Famien, the god of fertility, with important characters in the Islamic religion.

Slaves took their pagan gods with them to the New World. For example, in Cuba's Santeria religion, a mixture of Islam, Christianity and paganism, the war god Chango, (Shango in The Gambia), Vodun, or Voodoo, god of the dead, (Akovodun in The Gambia), and Ogun, god of smiths (Gu in the Gambia), all appear in their original form.

Politics and the economy

The dispute over territory between The Gambia and its larger, Francophone neighbour, was finally settled in a treaty between Britain and France in 1889. The Republic of The Gambia was established in 1970 after it was given self-government in 1963 and became independent from Britain in 1965. The 1982 Senegambia Confederation set up with Senegal to co-ordinate economic and defence affairs broke down in 1989.

Banjul is a deep-water port where most imports are landed and the UK is The Gambia's traditional and leading trading partner. There is very little industry except that of groundnut processing. The country has no railway and few roads. The Trans-Senegambian highway links both parts of Senegal through Farafenni, about halfway up-country. Banjul, the country's capital, is linked to Dakar by road to the north and to Ziguinchor, Senegal, in the south.

However, new first class roads have now been constructed from the airport direct

Agriculture

Farming occupies more than 80 per cent of The Gambia's population who grow rice, fruit and vegetables for food, and groundnuts and cotton for export. The country still is not self-sufficient in food and relies on imports, especially during times of drought. Apart from the export of groundnuts and groundnut products, The Gambia earns little else except from the growing tourist trade, which began in 1965, and duty on goods shipped between the northern and southern sectors of Senegal.

to the resort areas (about 15 minutes' drive), between Brikama via Gunjur to Kartong and from Barra to Kerewan in the north bank region of the country.

Flora and Fauna

In 1977 Sir Dawda Jarawa, Gambia's former president, introduced the 'Banjul Declaration' for the protection of the country's flora and fauna.

Although this is Africa, this tiny country has lost most of its larger wildlife, especially the elephant, buffalo and bigger deer species such as the eland, hartebeest and waterbuck. Several small deer, however, may be seen, like the Grimm's duiker, the oribi, and the sitatunga, whose feet are specially designed for the swamplands in which it lives. It is said that the last giraffe was seen in 1899, and both lions and leopards are very rare. The largest wild cats which the visitor might see are the civet, serval and genet.

Visitors who wish to see the lions and elephants synonymous with the continent, generally take an excursion into one of Senegal's vast National Parks like the Niokolo Koba.

There are crocodiles throughout the country, where you are never far from the river or a sacred crocodile pool. Species to be found include the Nile, West African Dwarf, pygmy, and rare Bottlenose varieties which might be seen on exposed mudflats, and there are a few hippopotami, especially further up the Gambia River. Here, vervet monkeys, patas monkeys, olive baboon troops, forest deer and warthogs can usually be spotted. Rarer are the colonies of red colobus monkeys which can sometimes be seen high in the taller trees bordering the river, and the even rarer Mona monkey.

Warthogs are not uncommon in The Gambia, but are often hard to spot because of their shy evasive nature, obviously learned from past experience as they make a fine roast! Aardvarks use their strong claws and long tongues to feed on termites in the numerous termite mounds dotting the landscape up-country, and jackals and spotted hyenas can often be heard at night.

A boat trip in the wide Gambia River estuary generally assures the sighting of the estuarine dolphins which inhabit the river as far up as

Chimpanzees' Half-way House

Up the river, on Baboon Island, an experiment has been going on for around 15 years to rehabilitate chimpanzees which have been retrieved from poachers and illicit animal dealers, into the wild. The public are not permitted to visit the island. However, the chimps might be seen from the river.

Albreda. Fishing is popular in the estuary and up-river, and around 18 varieties of gamefish can be caught here, some up to 300lbs in weight. The more popular game fish include tarpon, tuna, barracuda, catfish, ladyfish, and butterfish.

Apart from taking a river trip, the best way to see wildlife in its natural habitat is in the Abuko Nature Reserve and its tiny zoo. The zoo is near Banjul and contains around 50 species of local trees. Here the wildlife is rather disappointing. The few specimens include a lion, serval, baboons, vervet monkeys, the western red colobus monkeys, red patas monkeys, hyena, bushbuck, duiker,

striped ground squirrels, monitor lizards, crocodiles and several snakes including python, and the poisonous green mamba, cobra and puff adders. The zoo includes an animal orphanage, and a special crocodile pool. There is a hide on the two-kilometre walk from where many of the 280 species of birdlife in the reserve might be seen. A variety of butterflies also adds colour to this small area of carefully preserved jungle.

In the sandy grasslands outside the luxuriant river and poolside growth, the wildlife is sparse and of little interest. In contrast, the mangrove stands are hives of activity; fiddler crabs dart in and out of the mud around the tree roots, and small, edible oysters hang from the stumps which project through the water. Mudskippers, a fish which almost 'walks' on its fins, and the rare lungfish might be seen in the mangroves, and the canopy of tough-leaved branches above provides adequate nesting and perching for a great variety of bird life.

A new, and more natural nature reserve has been built several miles south from Banjul, on the Atlantic Coast. This location has been carefully selected to provide a cross-

Above: *Explore off the beaten track in a 4-wheel drive*

Far left: *This Western baboon might seem friendly, but it is the youth's pet!*

Left: *Gambia's markets attract vendors from across the country and even from Senegal*

section of environments, representing most of the country's natural habitats. Tanji Reserve has a beach and seashore with offshore sandbanks, mangrove, freshwater marshland, a river estuary, forest, and savannah. A replica Mandinka village has also been built here to educate Gambians and visitors about the early lifestyles of the country.

Inland, rock hydrax, a tiny relative of the elephant, jackals, pangolin, around 30 varieties of snake, geckos, lizards and scorpions inhabit a sparse, dry landscape dotted with doom palm, stands of kola palm, date groves, and towering termite

Groundnuts

Introduced to West Africa from South America by the Portuguese in the 16th century, *arachis hypoganea*, the groundnut, ground pea, peanut, or monkeynut, is an edible tuber. Originally developed commercially by the Governor of Dakar, Louis Faidherbe, in 1854, groundnut production quickly spread to The Gambia. Visitors will see vast heaps of collected groundnuts at many collection points up the Gambia River, in sacks often stacked as high as houses. Sadly, due to the unreliable river transport, much of the crop can rot and go to waste before collection.

mounds. Elephant grass and thorn scrub cover much of the landscape up-country. The giant mahogany tree is endemic here, as is the bamboo, used in domestic fencing, and the kapok, or silk-cotton tree.

In an attempt to protect what little wildlife Gambia has, six further areas are protected reserves and these include the Bijilo forest near the coast, the large Kiang West reserve, Nyambai, Furnyar, Kabafita and Salaji.

The Gambia has more bird life per acre than any other country. Sea and river birds abound, with a wide selection of waders, heron, of which there are seven varieties, pelicans, flamingos, storks, and nine varieties of kingfisher. These include the world's largest and smallest kingfishers, and the pied kingfisher. The curious hammerkop can often be seen on the riverbanks, as can darters and three varieties of egrets. The rare African fin-foot

Ornithology's tiny secret

The little enclave of The Gambia is a birdwatcher's paradise. A river trip reveals the extent of this small country's bird life which has been numbered at around 540 species, 150 of which are European migrants.

Part of the legume family, this plant thrives in quite arid conditions and is an ideal cash crop for this part of the world. A
nondescript plant above soil, the tubers develop underground
and the groundnut grows as a pea or bean, generally two, inside
each woody pod. The groundnut is an annual plant with a yearly
crop.

Peanuts are high in protein, creating an allergy in some people,
and are an integral part of western vegetarian diets and many
West African dishes. Grumpy soup (ground pea soup) is a local
favourite and groundnut sauce is used in many dishes. Groundnut oil is also prized for cooking, although most Africans prefer
the slightly rancid taste of palm oil. Products made from the nut
include refined oil, peanuts for eating raw or roasted, peanut
butter, and a soap made from the poorer quality oil. The locals
press the discarded groundnut shucks into a material used as a
fuel for cooking.

can also be seen here, as can
the scarce white-backed night
heron, and purple herons, cormorants, tree-ducks, and geese.

In the mangrove roots and
riverside undergrowth it may
be possible to spot one of three
varieties of plover, and both
sacred ibis and crane perch
above in the higher branches.

In the grasslands, especially
near wooded areas, or rice
fields, marabou storks are
common, as are weaver birds.
Blue-bellied rollers, the hoopoe, hornbills and parrots, like
the rose-necked parakeet, may
also be seen, and hotel grounds
are often the playground of
sunbirds, bee-eaters, orioles,
red-cheeked cordon-bleus,
and firefinches. Attentive

birdwatchers might catch a
glance of a Viellot's bearded
barbet, the spectacular violet
touraco, the amethyst starling,
or a green-backed Eremomela.

Larger birds like the kites and
vultures are common, but it
might not be so easy to catch a
glimpse of the rare harrier
eagle, fish eagle, or osprey, a
goshawk, or the lizard buzzard.
The Gambia has five types of
harrier, and two eagle varieties.
Other, more common bird
species include the palm nut
vulture, hooded, and white-
backed vulture, pied crows,
black magpies, grey-headed
gulls, Caspian terns, a variety of
pigeons, and three dove species.

(cont'd on page 41)

Tourism development

Tourism really took off in The Gambia during the 1970s when Europeans discovered just how close was this part of 'real' Africa and its winter sun. With a coastline of pure white sand, 80m (260ft) wide, stretching down the Atlantic shore for almost 35km (20 miles), this country offers an ideal climate with nine months a year of sunshine, in comfortable surroundings echoing with the sounds, sights and aromas of Africa.

The main tourist resort beaches are designated the Tourism Development Area (TDA) and the northern part has been tastefully developed for tourism activities. It is backed up by tropical river vegetation rich in bird life, unspoilt fishing and farming villages, and a traditional way of life with a fascinating heritage.

The Gambia Hotel Association was formed recently to promote tourism in conjunction with the Gambia Licensed Victualler's Association, which together monitor a large group of hotels, bars and restaurants.

There are now around 65 accommodations in The Gambia catering to all tastes and requirements. They range from luxury tourist and business hotels, to city hotels, beach hotels, guest houses, country hotels, rest houses and safari camps. Most tourists use the beach hotels fronting the long sandy coastline. There are around 25 of these, either on or very near the beach.

Probably one of the foremost tour operators to the Gambia is The Gambia Experience which has long been promoting tourism to the country in conjunction with the tourism authorities. It specialises not only in beach-side accommodation, but also offers a wide range of activities, tours and excursions which make the visitor's stay in The Gambia so much richer.

Opposite: The Sunwing Resort Hotel

38

For Further Information:

National Investment Promotion Authority
Independence Drive, Banjul
☎ (220) 228332, 228168, 229222, Fax: (220) 229220

Gambia Chamber of Commerce and Industry
P.O. Box 333, Banjul
☎ (220) 227042, 227765, Fax: (220) 229671

Gambia Hotels Association Atlantic Hotel, P.O. Box 296, Banjul ☎ (220) 228610, Fax: (220) 227861
Also, c/o **Bungalow Beach Hotel**, P.O. Box 2637, Serekunda ☎ 220 465288, 465623, Fax: 220 466 180

Gambia Licensed Victualler's Association
P.O. Box 270, Serekunda
☎ (220) 460929, 990929

The Gambia Experience
Kingfisher House,
Rownhams Lane,
North Baddesley,
Hampshire, SO51 8ZT U.K.
☎ 01703 730888

Black and White Safaris Ltd
Serekunda
☎ 393174, 393306

Gambia River Excursions
PO Box 664, Banjul
☎ 495526

Bush Safaris
Kotu Road, Kololi ☎ 70611

LA Creek Fishing
☎ 991313

Il Monda, ☎ 466573

West African Tours
☎ 495258

Gamtours, ☎ 392505

Five-Star Tours, ☎ 371110

Top Tips

Unless you are a back-packer or independent traveller with limited funds, or are staying in Banjul itself, you will be staying in a beach-side hotel in The Gambia. Naturally the glorious beaches of the Gambian coast are an attraction in themselves and will occupy most of your time here.

However, there is a wealth of interesting things to do and places to visit inland. Within a day, most of The Gambia's sites can be visited, although treks further up-river would include at least one night's stop-over. Possible visits to Senegal would involve a longer stay, although the nearer sites can be visited from Banjul in a one-day excursion. In this listing the symbol [*] indicates historic monuments; the symbol [**] indicates local life; and the symbol [***] indicates bird and wildlife.

Banjul [**]

The country's small capital city bustling with colourful markets, local places to eat and drink and sights to see such as its grand mosque, museum, old colonial houses, with streets lively with local traders and merchants.

Gunjur and Ghana Town [**]

Here, on wide expanses of sand, south of the beach hotels, hundreds of local fishermen draw up their colourful *pirogues* and divide up their Atlantic Ocean catch. In rows of large drying-huts, the fish are cured ready for distribution around the country.

Juffure and Albreda [*]

Across the wide Gambia River estuary, this is home to the story of Alex Haley's novel *Roots* and an insight into local village life, the nearby slave houses and ancient cannon bringing to mind the grim history of this part of West Africa.

Fort James [*]

In the middle of the wide Gambia River, the island fort's ruins and armaments bring to life the history of confrontations between the French and British, squabbling over the pickings of the slave trade.

Brikama [**]

This bustling market town is not far from the beaches but brings the African way of life into perspective with bustling stalls manned by locals in colourful robes offering craftwork, textiles and fruit and vegetables amongst the backdrop of native houses.

Lamin [***]

Located on a beautiful creek, Lamin village and Lamin Lodge offer not only a great diversity of wildlife and birdlife, but an insight into how local farmers live and carry on everyday life.

Tendaba [***]

A custom-built safari lodge, built near the River Gambia, from where the surrounding countryside can be explored and the wildlife and birdlife can be watched at leisure. River excursions by dug-out canoe are a speciality.

Kaur and Wassau [*]

Sites of the famous ancient standing stone circles which have mystified historians for centuries. Set in isolation, these historic monuments also spread into Senegal.

Georgetown [*]

This historic town is situated on MacCarthy Island in the middle of the River Gambia. Some old colonial buildings and slave houses remind one that this was a slave-trading centre. Today it is a lively market town.

The encroachment of the sandy Sahel, part of the southern reaches of the Sahara Desert, exacerbated by the relentless deforestation in the wake of the demand for firewood, has denuded much of The Gambia area away from the river.

The further east one travels, the more noticeable is the lack of vegetation. The severe lack of water and arid soil contributes to the bleak landscape and the majority of vegetation is found around settlements and villages where irrigation is possible. Otherwise, elephant grass, gaunt baobab, or 'upside down' trees, huge, stark kapok trees and thorn scrub is all that can survive in the harsh hinterland. However, where there is sufficient water, local farmers raise groundnuts, maize, rice, tomatoes, onions and other vegetables.

Flowers like hibiscus, leander, black-eyed susan, and the blooms of the flamboyant trees, endorse the fact that this is indeed a real tropical country. Butterflies add colour to the sometimes drab landscape, and occasionally vast swarms descend on small pools of fresh water to take a vital sip.

2 BANJUL AND ITS LOCALITY

Most visitors to The Gambia will arrive at Banjul International Airport, 20kms (12 miles) from Banjul, the country's capital. From the airport, visitors will generally travel directly to their beachside hotel without passing through the city. However, Banjul is easily reached by taxi or car from all the major hotels along the coast and is well worth a visit.

The Serekunda Highway leads into Banjul merging with the Old Cape Road from the beach hotels before passing over Denton Bridge. This is Banjul's only bridge, named after the Victorian Governor Denton. Crossing over the wide mouth of Oyster Creek, this bridge is a lively centre as it is also a jetty on the landward side for boats, *pirogues* and excursion craft. There has been a bridge here since 1879 and the present impressive structure which takes a dual carriageway,

Above: *Beautifully dressed women at Banjul's tourist craft market.*

was constructed in 1986. Around 3km (2 miles) on, past the turnings to the Wadner Beach Hotel and the Palm Grove Hotel, the road becomes Independence Drive, where the city begins.

Once called Bathurst, Banjul is one of the world's smallest capital cities. It is therefore easy to find one's way around the city and many of the roads are set out in a grid pattern. It is also easy to walk around the city in a couple of hours, longer if you browse leisurely through the many markets and shops.

Banjul is colourful and vibrant, bustling and busy, presenting the visitor with a crystallised slice of African life, unlike many other African cities. A visit to Banjul is a snapshot of real Gambian life that will whet your appetite to see more of the country.

Background

With a population of around 45,000, Banjul is even smaller than its two neighbouring towns, Serekunda and Bakau. This is due mainly to its location on a tiny peninsula at the end of a cape on a small, flat island known as St. Mary's Island, originally named Banjul (Bam-

Banjul

The city originated in 1816 as a British Royal Naval base from which to harass foreign slave trading vessels. The capital was named after the Colonial Secretary of the time, Earl Bathurst (1762-1834). However, the country was still in dispute between the British and the French, who were based in Albreda on the north bank of the river. Britain finally claimed The Gambia in 1888, but it was still administered from nearby Sierra Leone until Bathurst officially became The Gambia's capital in 1892. It changed its name to Banjul upon Independence in 1965.

boo). This projects out into the wide mouth of the Gambia River, with Banjul port facing the ferry landing of Barra on the northern riverbank opposite.

Because it was founded relatively recently, there are few really historic sites in Banjul.

The naval base was quickly occupied by merchants and traders in the mid-19th century when the large **Albert Market** was built on Russell Street. This multi-level wooden building which housed an 'Aladdin's Cave' of stalls, was destroyed by fire in 1986. It was replaced in 1993 with a more modern market, nearer the Atlantic Hotel.

As Banjul is a major port, not only for the export of groundnuts, the country's main produce, but also for the import of most consumer goods, the city is a centre for all kinds of merchandising.

The **Barra Ferry** which plies between the south and north banks of the Gambia River links the city to the road which leads through Senegal to that country's capital, Dakar. This is also an important trading route and numerous merchants come down to Banjul from Dakar to trade in the city. For this reason the markets of Banjul are stocked with a bewildering variety of goods from handicrafts, paintings and furniture, to fruit and vegetables and electrical goods, and from watches and perfumes to bolts of colourful cloth.

A great deal of fabric is shipped through Banjul, and there are many clothes stalls and tailor's shops which can run up any item of clothing bespoke.

Touring Banjul

It is usually from the Albert Market that most visitors begin to find their way around this small city. The entire city is no more than a couple of kilometres from north to south, or from the Atlantic Hotel to the docks.

Compact as it is, Banjul is divided into six areas. **Portuguese Town** is to the north, behind the beach; **New Town** lies between this and the marshy southern limits of the city; **Soldier Town** is to the east and **Mocam Town** lies behind it. **Jollof Town** encompasses the wharf area and portside buildings and **Half Die** is a semi built-up area on the southern tip of the island on which Banjul stands. The open, stagnant drains in this area remind one that Half Die is named in memory of the victims of a cholera epidemic which swept the city in 1869. However, these divisions are rather academic, as is the fact that some streets have recently been renamed, a fact that has little significance as there are few street name signs!

Albert Market, on Russell Street, could well be called the city centre as it is the focus of much of Banjul's activity. Next to the market are the Gamtel telephone exchange and the city's post office. On Wellington Street, just south of the site of Albert Market, towards the Barra Ferry Terminal, is a fine craft market known as the **Tourist Market**, where gold and silver jewellery, wood carvings, batik, tie-dye textiles and leather goods like handbags and belts can be purchased. African music cassettes can also be bought at a shop in this market or at Kerewan Sound, stall number 5 in Albert Market itself.

> ## *Bargain entertainment*
> Whatever you intend to buy in the markets or shops, try haggling over the price as this can not only save money, but can be quite entertaining!

Across from Albert market is the open space of the **Mac-Carthy Square,** usually bald of grass through lack of irrigation. Cricket is sometimes played on this rather unsightly square. A World War I memorial stands in the south-east corner of the square. A small bandstand, and government buildings called the Quadrangle, built much in the same manner as a traditional prep school in England, face the square which is often ringed by the stalls of itinerant traders.

A path leads down from the Quadrangle to the Six-Gun Battery where 24-pounders still stand. Across from Mac-Carthy Square, to the west, on Independence Drive, is the tiny Anglican **Cathedral of St. Mary**. This Victorian, corrugated iron roofed church sports a slender spire and has some interesting British military memorial plaques.

Near here is the city's only museum. The **National Museum** contains an unusual collection of archaeological, historic and ethnographic interest. Although the exhibits are rather scant, there are some fine examples of old maps, photographs, tribal dolls, masks, wood carvings, pottery, pots, African weapons and early guns, an exhibition of palm-wine making history, examples of *warri* boards (the local game), and a curious Iron-Age wood drill. Opposite the Museum is the city taxi stand (Open: 8.00-16.00 Monday-

Thursday, 8.00-13.00 Friday & Saturday).

A short walk away, just back from Independence Drive, the gated pink and white **State House** with its sentry post is a fine example of colonial architecture with verandas, shutters, immaculate gardens and flagpole.

Other architectural gems can be found just by diverting off the wide main streets. These are the balconied and shuttered, wooden 'Creole'-style houses, built during Victorian times, often raised on concrete pillars and sporting corrugated iron roofs. Both bungalows and two-storied buildings, many are now in a dismal state of repair but most retain their early elegance. Much of Banjul is rather 'Shanty-townish', with family compounds of single-storied, corrugated iron and stone huts.

The most striking building, located on Box Bar Road to the west of the city, is the gleaming new **Banjul Central Mosque**, or King Khaled Mosque. Built in 1988, this magnificent structure has taken over as the city's main mosque from one built of breeze blocks in the 1930s at the north end of Mosque Road, and an even earlier model on the same site built of grass in the 1870s. This mosque is still known as the Great Mosque. Although there are several smaller mosques in the city, the spectacular structure of the Khaled Mosque far outshines any other building in the city, even the earlier **Catholic Cathedral**. This stands on the corner of Picton and Hagan Streets in the centre of the city, and contains interesting wooden ceilings and ornate windows. Opposite the cathedral is the San Rafael Snackbar.

Saved from the flood

South of the Khaled Mosque is a road fronting mudflats known as Crab Island. During a potential flood in 1947, a Muslim holy man, or Imam, prayed on this site to abate the tide. The waters receded, Banjul was saved, and the Imam gave his name to the road - Imam Omar Sowe.

Box Bar Road, named after the 1862 sluice gate on the site, runs down the eastern limits of the city to Independence Drive. On Box Bar Road, opposite the southern corner of the Khaled Mosque compound, is Jobe Jewellers, excellent for gold and silver filigree work.

Above: These colourfully-decorated, sea-going pirogues annually compete in an animated Senegalese boat-race

Left: Craft stalls have proliferated in The Gambia since the author was first there thirty years ago

Eating and more

Because of the trading legacy of the city, Banjul is a cosmopolitan mixture of ethnic creeds and colours. Tall, dark, Mauritanian Tuaregs in light blue robes, mainly silver traders, mix with Gambian businessmen in tie-dye 'Gambishirts' and haughty Berbers in white *burnous*; Rastafarians in

Above: Remember to remove your shoes if you want to see inside Banjul's Great Mosque

brightly-coloured woollen hats man stalls alongside the generously proportioned Mandinka women, in flowing local costume, selling a daunting selection of spices and peppers. A few Germans, Danes, Indians and Lebanese have set up businesses in the city generally selling electrical goods or running restaurants. There are a few excellent, if comparatively basic, eating houses in the city.

Probably one of the more salubrious is the **African Heritage** on Wellington Street where the restaurant doubles as a commendable art gallery and shop. The German-Lebanese run **Braustuble** is a courtyard-style restaurant with excellent food and a well-stocked circular bar near the Quadrangle on Leman Street. Lebanese food, especially snacks, can also be found on Cameron Street and, in the back streets there are several stalls called *tangana*, or chop-stalls, often just a table set up on a vacant lot.

The Oasis Shawarma Restaurant between Clarkson and Hagan Streets is also a nightclub and is next to Uncle Joe's Bar on Cameron and Dobson Streets. Across the roundabout from Uncle Joe's is the Phase One Bar. This latter bar stands at the east end of Albion Place and, four blocks west, in the western corner of Albion Place, is the Caribbean Bar, on Allen and Ingram Streets, and the Joe Bassy Restaurant.

Just around the corner from here, to the west, on Hope Street and Sam Jack Terrace, is the Duma Guest House. Sam Jack Terrace, named after a Gambian Speaker of the House of Representatives, leads down to the Museum on Independence Drive where there is the International Fast Food Café and minibus park. Not far from the Duma Guest House, on Fitzgerald and Grant Streets is another small hotel, the Abbey. Other local chop houses are the Gambia and the Ngalam Afric Bar.

Peanut vendors are common and vendors sometimes wander the streets selling titbits. Food and drink is inexpensive in the city but if you require European surroundings and food, go to the city's main hotel, the Atlantic, on Marine Parade. You will pass the Royal Victoria Hospital, the UN Building, Banjul City Council and the National Assembly offices, between Marine Parade and Independence Drive.

If you carry on along the Drive, you will come to the Carlton Hotel and the Kantora

Hotel with the Whole World snack bar in between. **The Atlantic Hotel** is the oldest-established hotel in the Gambia and is a ten-minute walk from the city centre, two minutes from the Carlton Hotel. This hotel has a beach and pool and well-maintained gardens; poolside snacks are provided or a full à la carte meal in the restaurant. Between the Atlantic Hotel and the Albert Market is the Town Beach – not advisable if you don't want to be pestered by local beach-bums.

Away from the bustle

For those who wish to explore a little more of this tiny city, take a walk down from the Albert Market, south, along Wellington Street. On the right, just up Cameron Street there is the Burger House and the Samburger Restaurant on opposite sides of the road. Continue south, past the CFAO Store, the African Heritage Restaurant, the Banjul Pharmacy on the next block, and the little Adonis Hotel, to the **Barra Ferry Terminal** and docks on Wellington Street. Just before the ferry terminal, on the left, is the mustering point for canoes and boats which can be hired

to Barra Point or for Creek Excursions.

Almost opposite the ferry terminal, on Buckle and Orange Streets, is the Apollo Hotel; the Brikamba Hotel is also on Buckle Street. A block down is Cotton Street. This is an area of old warehouses and storage compounds and the Bus Station, on the sandy King George V Park.

Relics of war

During World War II, hangars in King George V Park housed Sunderland flying boats used in anti-submarine warfare and around 100 anti-aircraft guns, never fired in anger, were also sited here.

Continuing up Cotton Street to Bund Road, the city is gradually left behind as mud-flats take over. Because of its isolation, it is best to go with a companion or in a group. The hulks of old boats and the sudden quiet create a curious contrast to the bustle of the city just a few minutes away.

(cont'd on page 52)

For traditional Gambian cuisine, you might try the Calypso beach bar at Cape Point or, for Italian dishes, Luigi's Restaurant and La Valbonne are worth a try.

Pizzas and pasta dishes are served at the Al'Italiana Restaurant. The Neptune and Al Basha restaurants serve Lebanese food, and the Scala Restaurant has an extensive Danish menu.

For Chinese Szechwan and Cantonese food, the Panda Restaurant is good, and the Tao specialises in South East Asian food. In the Kotu Stream area, there are two Chinese restaurants near the Police Station, the Panda, and the Canton restaurants. There are also two other Chinese restaurants in the Fajarah area. These are the Yellow Gate, and the Golden Dragon restaurants.

If you require food with the French touch, then try the Ngala Lodge, and, for an à la carte menu, The Dunda, at the Atlantic Hotel, or the Flamingo Restaurant in the Senegambia hotel are both heartily recommended.

4th Dimension
next to Senegambia Hotel
☎ 460709

African Heritage
Liberation Avenue, Banjul
☎ 226906

APGWA Restaurants, Mini Markets, Fashion Shop
74 Kombo Sillah Drive, Churchills
☎ 392826

Amsterdam Dolphins
Serekunda Road, near
Palma Rima Hotel ☎ 460590

Athina
Kairaba Avenue, Fajara ☎ 392638

Bacchus
Mile 2 Beach, Banjul ☎ 227948

Bakadaji
near Palma Rima Hotel ☎ 462307

Bamba Dinka
Atlantic Road, Bakau

Bamboo
Fajara ☎ 495764

Braustable
77 OAU Boulevard, Banjul
☎ 228371

Bull and Bush Steakhouse
Kairaba Avenue

Centrepoint Restaurant
4 Daniel Goddard Street, Banjul
☎ 228378

Churchill's Bar and Restaurant
near Palma Rima Hotel
☎ 460830

Clay Oven Indian
Old Cape Road ☎ 496600

Di'Vino
near Senegambia Hotel
☎ 460929

El Basha
near Senegambia Hotel
☎ 463300

Flying Dutchman
Kololi Beach, Kololi ☎ 460099

Fransisco's
Fajara, Atlantic Road, off
Kairaba Avenue ☎ 495332

Grand Café Tussen Zussen Bar and Restaurant
Senegambia, Kololi

Il Mondo
near Bungalow Beach Hotel,
Kotu ☎ 466573

Le Lotus
110 Kairaba Avenue, Fajara
☎ 496026

Le Valbonne
Kololi Beach, Kololi ☎ 460247

Luigi's Pizza
next to Palma Rima Hotel
☎ 460280

MacFadis Restaurant
61 Kairab Avenue, Fajara
☎ 390412

Madeline's Inn
Kairaba Avenue, Fajara
☎ 391464

Neptuno
opposite Palma Rima Hotel
☎ 460434

Oasis
1 Clarkson Street, Banjul and
76 Cape Point Road, near
Sunwing Hotel ☎ 497737

Paradise
next to Bungalow
Beach Hotel, Kotu ☎ 466246

Sambous
Old Cape Road, Bakau
☎ 495237

Scala
Kololi Beach, Kololi ☎ 46813

Seaview Beach Bar and Restaurant
Senegambia Beach, Kololi
E-mail seaview@hotmail.com

Sir William
Kotu Stream ☎ 466111

Solomon
near Palma Rima Hotel
☎ 460716

Tam-Tam
opposite Badala Park Hotel,
Kotu Stream ☎ 464922

The Dolphine
next to Kairaba Hotel
☎ 460929

The Grilled Fish
51 Kairaba Avenue, Fajara
☎ 374865

The Italian
Kololi Beach, Kololi ☎ 460063

The Mango Tree
Kololi Highway ☎ 460895

Weezo's and La Cantina
Kairaba Avenue, Fajara
☎ 496918

Yvonne Class
Cape Point, Bakau ☎ 495888

Bund Road actually follows a dyke which encircles the southern side of the entire city of Banjul running alongside a creek, Crab Island Fish Pond. The creek divides the city from the mainland but, if you are walking, it is a long three kilometre (2mile) walk. It is best to return to Banjul where you can take a meal or a taxi could be found to return to your hotel.

Barra, Fort Bullen and the north coast

For those visitors to Banjul with time to spare and a wish to see a little more of Gambia life and a snippet of history, a ferry trip across the mouth of the Gambia River is an interesting option. Two hundred people of a wondrous mixture of races, colours, trades and persuasions are ferried backwards and forwards across the river to the north bank where the Banjul to Dakar highway begins its 20 mile trek across northern Gambia and the 200 mile journey to Dakar, Senegal's capital.

Once on dry land one is in what is basically a vast lorry park with a local restaurant and sprawling market. Many items can be bought here more

Barra ferry

Just mingling with the passengers, cars, lorries, bicycles and livestock being shipped over the water to Barra, is an experience in itself. There are seven daily sailings of the ferry which takes 30 minutes to cross the wide estuary. The ferry sailing is very cheap for the foot passenger and the views of the city and the river mouth are worth the trip. The tidal estuary here is one of Africa's largest at 19km (12 miles).

cheaply than in the markets of Banjul. There is little to attract the sightseer here at the Barra ferry landing except the bustle of colourful local people, the market and the groundnut loading station.

However, the attractions of **Barra** for the visitor, including the fact that it was once the old capital of the Mandinka Kingdom, hold no interest for the African travellers on the ferry. Turning left from the rickety landing stage and through the lorry park onto a dusty road, a signpost points the short distance to **Fort Bullen**. You will pass two rather scruffy guest houses, the Lingaire Hotel near the ferry dock and the Rest House, near the fort.

An official guide will appear once you get to the site of the fort which stands on a headland looking out towards the blue Atlantic Ocean. The spot is isolated, deserted apart from the guide, and quite exposed. **Be sure to bring water with you as there is also little shelter and keep to the pathways, as it is known that there are snakes in the grass and scrubland**. This caution should be borne in mind wherever you walk in Africa, especially in places like this which are relatively undisturbed.

This now ruined fort was built by the British in 1826 to protect the trading route of the Gambia River and repel any attacks on what was Bathurst, now Banjul, on the opposite side of the river estuary. A few ramparts, crumbling turrets and toppled rusting cannon lie around the historic site. There is a small beach here and a guard post, but little else remains of one of The Gambia's earliest fortresses. **Remember, the last ferry back to Banjul leaves Barra at 18.30.**

The coast north of Barra, a 6km (4 mile) sweep of beaches, is practically unexplored and virgin. Taking the dusty road north, towards the Senegal border, this part of the Trans-Senegambian Highway cuts inland, away from the coast to the border town of Amdallai, on the Gambian side, and Karang on the Senegalese side. West of these border posts there is the area known as **Jinek**. This is almost a large island, the top of which is actually in Senegal territory.

Jinek can be reached by Land Rover from Barra, a bumpy journey followed by a short canoe trip across the river tributary at Niji. Alternatively, a boat to the island can be chartered from Banjul. On the Atlantic side of the island is a cluster of thatched huts known as the **Madiyana Bush Camp**. There is little to do on Jinek except laze in the sun or go beachcombing on the pure white sands. You can stay at this remote resort, which has a bar-restaurant, no generator and little else. As everything has to be imported by boat from Banjul, except the marijuana which is discretely cultivated nearby, it is important to book your accommodation in advance.

Above left: *Early gun emplacement, Fort Bullen*

Above right: *The Gambia's national flag leads this boat excursion*

Below: *Hitching a ride the traditional way!*

A typical Gambian town

Many visitors are rather apprehensive when first visiting a local African village and its bustling market. There is no need to feel nervous unless you are visiting a rather remote town, where a foreign face might attract interest, purely out of curiosity. In most Gambian towns you can feel safe – there is little crime - but, as in every busy street anywhere in the world, be sensible about how you carry your wallet, valuables or handbag.

There are several things to remember. Take time, do not rush, bargain when buying anything; the Gambians can spend a whole day haggling over one purchase! Do not take photographs blatantly without first asking, or just gesturing for an assent. Above all, remember that this is home to the locals, not just a tourist sideshow. Each village and town in Senegambia is a microcosm of everyday African life.

Approaching a typical Gambian township like **Serekunda** or **Brikama**, one initially has the feeling of entering a higgledy-piggledy maze of one-storey corrugated iron shacks, spreading each side of a wide dirt road. The smells of fruit, vegetables, woodsmoke, diesel fumes, cooking and more natural odours combine with the colour of local costumes and bright bolts of cloth for sale, suddenly to assail the nostrils and eyes. From each side of the road, transistor radios and cassette players blare forth.

Many of the shacks facing into the road with open doorways and awning shades, are shops, often with local wares displayed on rude tables in front of the doorways. Traffic, bicycles ringing bells, honking cars, overloaded bush taxis, lorries, wooden trolleys, long-horned-oxen carts and rickety donkey-drawn vehicles seem to jostle each other for position, only just avoiding the crowds of shoppers and sightseers who occasionally drift into the path of the passing traffic.

The initial impression of the town might seem chaotic but there is, however, a purpose both to the apparent disorder and to the town's layout, which is not immediately appreciated. Make first for the centre of the village or town, generally the widest part of the dirt-sand main street. In most towns, which have grown up from being small villages many centuries ago, there is a central point designated for the meetings of revered village elders. Although the police and government deal with most major issues, the elders, and often the Islamic Imam or priest, still oversee local issues.

A large, ancient kapok or baobab tree is the traditional focal point of every West African village. Often they are many centuries old and not difficult to spot in the village or town centre. It is under these trees that the elders will gather to sort out local social issues and any small disputes. Sometimes wooden benches have been constructed around the huge trunks of this tree. You will often see locally painted notices advertising social events, meetings or even local wrestling matches, pinned to these trees which are still regarded as sacred.

The Mosque

Since the advent of Islam, the mosque has become the central religious point of most villages. The local mosque reflects the town's wealth and can be anything from a small mud-bricked hut, denoted by the crescent symbol of Islam on its roof, or the colourful flags flying from its compound walls. The flags are often green or black, the colours of Islam. Up-country you will see a variety of mosque designs, many of which will sport either a minaret which can be climbed (and from the top of which the Imam, or Muslim priest, calls the faithful to prayer), an ornamental minaret, or a spire.

You will note that however ornate the decorations on the mosque, there are no carvings or decorations representing animals, humans or plants. This is because Islam forbids the representation of any living thing in architectural decoration. Instead, the decorations are geometric, or comprised of stylised writing, texts from their holy book the Koran, or representations of their prophet's name, Mohammed. Wolof, Sarakole, Tukulor and Mandinka tribes are all devoutly and predominantly Muslim.

In Serekunda you will also notice two Christian churches, as The Gambia is both Islamic and Christian. Christ's Church in Serekunda, was once just a wartime hut, and the few churches up-river, like those at Georgetown and Basse Santa Su, were designed initially as mission schools.

There are several Christian charities in The Gambia which run schools, missions and medical stations. In The Gambia, it is mainly the Serer and Diola tribes who adhere to the Christian beliefs.

Animism

The third religion in The Gambia is Animism, which is still very powerful. You will see many people wearing amulets, or *gris-gris*, on their arms, around their necks or around the ankles. These are often little leather boxes, or cowrie shells, containing some sacred scrap of parchment, spell or charm, which is said to protect the wearer. These amulets will have been provided, either at birth, or on initiation, by the local *griot*, or Animist priest. However, many Gambian Animists hedge their bets by belonging to either a Christian church or Islam as well as worshipping the spirits of their ancestors and those of trees, weather, earth, water or war!

The Marketplace

The central commercial point of each town is the open market. Many of these marketplaces are organised, each stallholder having his, or generally her, own spot. In some towns the market might be custom-built from bricks and corrugated iron. Others might just have large cloth awnings spread over the stalls, supported by wooden props.

Generally it is the Gambian women who dominate in the markets, and you will usually be able to pick out the stout, colourfully-dressed women with elaborate head-dresses who appear to control a number of stalls. The markets are generally divided into separate areas: one where colourful spices and herbs and local remedies are sold, another area devoted to dried and fresh fish, one to meat, another to vividly exotic vegetables and

Market traders

You will see a wide gamut of tribespeople represented in the typical local market: tall, elegant Fulani; haughty, handsome and very dark Wolof; Malinke sporting massive gold earrings; Berbers and Tuaregs in voluminous blue or white robes and black turbans; Serer, the largest ethnic group, with intricately woven hairpieces; and Peuls, herding their prized Zebu cattle into the market enclosures.

fruit, yet another to lavishly patterned cloth and clothing, another to household items, and one area to livestock.

Local women shop carefully, bargaining and haggling over each purchase, often for a long time, sometimes with a sleeping baby strapped to their backs with a long length of batik or tie-dyed cloth. Women can come to Serekunda market to peddle their wares from great distances, often having to walk miles to the nearest road and then take a bush taxi into town. All this, balancing a heavy bowl or bucket of fruit, fish, bolts of cloth, bundles of firewood, or home-made craftwork on their heads.

The marketplace is not the only place to shop as the stores facing the main streets offer all kinds of goods and services, from butchers to barber shops, from bars and roadside take-aways, known as chop-houses, to local doctors' surgeries and dentists, to stores selling handicraft, baskets, earthenware cooking pots, metalwork and even fortune tellers' services. You can find somebody offering almost any service from bicycle mending to enamel dish repairs, from gold and silversmiths who will make jewellery to order, to tailors, usually working at their old-fashioned sewing machines outside their workshops, who will also make clothes to order.

Bengdulas

Several shops may sell souvenirs, such as the bengdulas, where you can watch expert wood carvers turning logs of hardwood into antelopes, elephants, hippos, masks, exaggerated native figures,

Above: Friendly faces...

Left: Wash your hands after touching hot chillis!

Below: An up-country trek sets out

or useful items like bowls and wooden knives, spoons and forks with elaborate handles. Some sell colourful beads, glass, amber, clay or necklaces made from seeds. Exquisite gold and silver filigree work can also be found, and leather workers fashion bags, belts and household items with intricate patterns. Start haggling by offering a third of the price first asked. Look for the hand-painted naive shop signs, advertising all sorts of wares and services, that make interesting and occasionally amusing photographs.

Homes and workshops

Behind the bustle of the main streets are the townspeople's homes and workshops. There is little apparent order to the layout of towns or villages. This is because they will have spread out over the centuries from being very small villages or even a single family homestead. Alternatively, as in Banjul or Georgetown up-river, colonial settlers designed the town on a grid system when they established it. The large, white-painted and brick-built houses of the more wealthy can back onto the lowliest of hovels. Most houses are roofed with corrugated iron, but sometimes the older houses will be rondavel-style with a thatched roof.

Most families, generally extended families with several genera-tions, live in what are known as compounds. These can be any size and are enclosures made of corrugated iron, plaited straw or bamboo, mud walls or thorn brushwood, that contain the ex-tended family's communal home, with a yard for recreation, cooking, winnowing rice and millet, keeping livestock and a well or iron drum for water. There are also public wells in the towns, many provided by an Islamic Trust in Saudi Arabia. With the older, round, thatched huts, cooking might be done inside, with the smoke being expelled through a hole in the roof.

Many compounds are large enough for the family's livestock, which generally include a cow and goats for milk and meat, chicken, and sometimes a pet dog or even a parrot. The com-pound might also have a vegetable patch and fruit trees like orange, paw-paw, guava, mango or banana. It may also include a place were work is done, such as a place for dyeing and drying tie-dye or batik cloth, a spot for making clay and earthenware pots, or weaving cloth. In every compound you will see the traditional wooden pestle and mortar, much larger than those in the average western kitchen!

Schools and Games

You will also see the local schools. Generally the primary schools are run by an Imam, or Islamic holy man, from his home. Here he will teach excerpts from the Koran, or Islamic Bible. For a small donation, children will recite sayings from Mohammed, the Muslim's first prophet. On a blackboard, the Imam will write verses in Arabic, which the children will copy and learn by rote. Because there is a shortage of writing materials, the children will use an improvised slate made of a board of palm wood and a piece of charcoal. When the text is no longer needed, the light-coloured surface of the board is cleaned by scrubbing with sand.

Older children will attend a state run primary and secondary school, generally custom-built, where they will learn all subjects, including the national language English. Few schoolbooks and a shortage of teaching aids mean that one class may learn from one very old textbook. However, you will notice that school-children are extremely

Children's games

Apart from children playing games of tag around the marketplace and in and out of the traffic, look closely at the games they are playing and you will see typical local ingenuity. You cannot buy children's toys in shops in The Gambia, so children and parents make their own from whatever scrap material is available: wooden spinning tops, tin cans fashioned into little model cars with wooden wheels, dolls made from straw, marbles fashioned from clay or stones, bowling hoops made from old bicycle wheel rims, and a whole range of discarded items doubling as a football!

proud of their school uniform and turn out spotlessly clean. They may have to walk several miles to attend the nearest school.

You may also see groups of men sitting on the sheltered wooden benches found dotted around the town, playing the national board game. This ancient game, dating from ancient Egypt, is known as *warri* in The Gambia. It is played in a similar way to backgammon. A wooden board, about half a metre long, has two rows of six cups carved into the surface. These cups are receptacles for the peas, or stones, which represent the pieces on the board. Sometimes these *warri* boards are ornately carved, often with an integral stand, and make ideal souvenirs.

One of the busiest gathering points in Serekunda is the bush taxi park where the gaudily-painted big estate cars and minibuses leave for the journey up-country. There is generally a bush taxi park in most Gambian towns, and especially at ferry landings like Barra. Here, local people and also those from far away in colourful costumes, Senegalese, Mauritanians, Moors and other nationalities, haggle over prices with bush taxi drivers, or discuss last minute business deals before the long ride home. Others clamber with unbelievable agility on board, still balancing a brightly-painted enamel dish loaded with purchases or goods wrapped in patterned cloth on their heads. Kola nut sellers, cigarette vendors and drink and sweetmeat merchants offer essentials for the journey up-river.

Wandering into the side streets you might hear somebody practising one of the region's local musical instruments. Brikama is a good place to hear the playing of the *kora*, a cross between a lute and a harp. Many celebrated *kora* players live in Brikama and will happily demonstrate the art of playing this local instrument. In every town and village there are reputable drum-players. Ask about the numerous styles, shapes and sizes of the traditional drums, and ask about their particular place in the Gambian ensemble and their historic significance.

There is certainly much more to the typical Senegambian town than one would initially think by just driving through the main street.

3 THE GAMBIAN COAST

This is the nearest English-speaking, tropical African beach resort to Europe. Brilliant white, crystal sandy beaches stretch 64km (40 miles) down from The Gambia's capital, Banjul, south, to the borders of Senegal. Stretching down along this coast, a string of hotels has sprung up over the last 30 years attracting tourists, mostly from Europe, to either bask on the sand and by the swimming pools, or take treks into The Gambia's interior. Hotels now extend about 8km (5 miles) along this idyllic coastline. However, the few hotels which have been built, do nothing to interrupt the wide expanse of sand where visitors can walk undisturbed as far as they like.

Above: *Kotu Beach*

The Guinea Current washes the beaches in warm Atlantic waters, combining with the north-east Trade Winds which cool the coast of Africa's most westerly shores.

At some points the sand is broken by creeks and waterways, known as *bolongs*, but after the strip of developed beach, coastal jungle foliage edges the sand dunes and fishing villages encroach on the shore. It is after passing one of the last tourist resort accommodations, the Kololi Beach Club, that the real Gambia begins.

Gambia beach-watch

For those visitors who are expecting a beach holiday in The Gambia comparable to that in the Caribbean or The Canaries, think twice. Certainly most hotels are located along the fine, wide strip of powdery sand which runs from Banjul down to Senegal, but the beach is undeveloped. Only 5 miles of The Gambia's 25 mile long stretch of beach, is bordered by hotels. None of these are more than three stories high, the height of a palm tree, and hotels are spread out in landscaped grounds, not crammed together. There are no ice-cream huts, deck-chair hire or watersports like paragliding, boat-hire, scuba diving and jet skiing, cluttering up the fine sand. Many hotels have gardens that run down to the beach, where sun-seekers can take towels and deck-chairs onto the strand. However, most tourists prefer the poolside to the beach.

This is not because the beach is unattractive. It is virginal white and beautiful, with dunes and scalloped bays edged with palms. Apart from the local hawkers and peddlers pestering relaxing visitors at every opportunity, the sea is not for the timid. This is the Atlantic Ocean and the current and waves have travelled thousands of miles before they dump their breakers on Gambia's shores. The waves can be huge, and almost impossible to swim in. The coastal sand also shelves off very near the water's edge, and the undertow can be treacherous.

This is also an ocean with a variety of marine life, including sharks, which the locals catch in great numbers. As there is no coral reef off

Gambia's coast, and the water close to the shore is very deep, sharks are not deterred from approaching a few yards offshore. Here, even paddlers should be wary of thorn-backed rays, jellyfish, poisonous stone fish and spiny sea urchins which can be concealed in the shallows or washed up to the water's edge. However, there are often wonderful shells and some fascinating driftwood and flotsam thrown up on the sand.

This all sounds rather daunting, but it is best to be aware of what to expect, however unlikely. One should not be put off the beach altogether. The beach is an ideal thoroughfare, and it is a delight to stroll down the coast towards the border with Senegal, watching the colourful fishing boats launched through the crashing waves or pulling up on the fine sand, and to see the assortment of fish unloaded and sorted.

There are also several fishing villages at intervals along the coast. Here, fish are sun-dried and cured. These villages often spill over onto the beach, and are always a hive of colourful activity. In the drying sheds and on the sorting tables you can see the great variety of fish which are caught in these waters. Walking along the beach is a pleasure, apart from peddlers who should be politely avoided. A few tiny beachside shacks offer an appetising selection of fish dishes.

Watch the small herds of large-horned *Zebu* cattle

Filming the catch

Women in bright native costumes arrive as if by magic when a fishing boat appears on the horizon, all balancing great enamel bowls on their heads. As the fish are tossed out of the boats, the women and fishermen haggle over the catch, down to the smallest minnow. Often the women will come away with massive fishes balanced in their bowls, head and tail dangling either side. You might even see a few shark among them. The whole procedure is immensely photogenic.

being brought down to the beach by the herdsboy, from the neighbouring fields. Why are they herded to the beach? The cattle lick vital salt from the rocks and beachside plants, an essential element in The Gambia's tropical heat, and this is their only natural source. Even humans should consider taking a little more salt with their food, as it replaces that lost in perspiration.

Strolling in the midday sun, one should be amply protected from sunburn; head cover is recommended, and sandals should be worn as the sand can often be too hot for bare feet. Away from the hotels and hawkers, one can usually find a secluded spot, behind a dune, to sunbathe. As this is mainly a Muslim country, topless sunbathing is frowned upon, but it is possible with discretion. The beach is also the best place at sundown, as the fiery African sunsets are spectacular.

The hotel strand

However, let us look first at the beachside tourism developments where you will probably be staying. As these hotels are the main accommodation for visitors to The Gambia, it is a good idea to get an impression of what is on offer along this part of the coast. Up-river, in the interior of the country, there is little accommodation to compare with that on the coastline.

Just out of Banjul, one leaves behind the city centre hotels like the Carlton, the Adonis and the Apollo, for

Boat hire

A short distance on from Wadner Beach Hotel, with Toll Point to the right, the road then crosses the Denton Bridge over Oyster Creek. Boat excursions into the Gambia River estuary and up-river, often commence at this bridge, which has a number of small jetties and yacht moorings. Fishermen can also hire boats for trips out into the creeks and estuary, or out to sea to fish for barracuda, shark, grouper, ladyfish and rays.

Above: The Atlantic Hotel

Left: Fish smokerie at Tanji

Bottom left: Local Zebu cattle

Bottom right: One of The Gambia's glorious beaches

the beachside Atlantic Hotel. The road crosses the salt mud-flats encircling the city, and passes the Palm Grove and Wadner Beach hotels on the stretch of beach parallel to the road, before the creek estuary.

The beaches on which most hotels are located extend from **Cape Point**, west and south in a line of scalloped bays interspersed by head-lands. These include the beaches of Bakau, Fajara Beach, Kotu Strand, Kotu Point, Kololi Beach and Kololi Point. There are around twenty hotels along the coast, many of which are on their own beaches or have access to a beach. In from the coast road there are many guest houses and motels where accommoda-tion is inexpensive. Running from north to south along the coast, the beach hotels and main points of interest are described first.

From the Banjul road, divert right, onto Old Cape Road. There is a short wooded area with Radio Gambia on Sait Matty Road which runs paral-lel, to the left, before the coast road is reached.

The first part of the coast fronts a local town called **Bakau**. On the right hand side there is a restaurant off the road called the 'Clay Oven'. There are two other restaurants on this part of the road, the Sambou's and Kias Fastfood; both have bars.

As the road curves around a headland here, to the right again is the residential centre of Bakau. There is a fine **Botanical Garden** off to the right, where prehistoric cyclands and other rare plants can be seen, but the coast road here turns to the left. Before Bakau, to the right, on the point, known as Cape Point, and overlooking the sea are the Cape Point Hotel, the Amies Beach Aparthotel and the Sunwing Hotel, all with good beach facilities. In the grounds of the Sunwing Hotel is the tomb of the Imam Sait Matty Bah, son of the King of Sene Saloum.

Part of the first section of the coastline from Cape Point is fronted by steep cliffs with either steps or paths leading down to fine sandy beaches. Just south of the Cape Point peninsula is a pretty, red laterite-cliffed bay where the tiny St. Peter's Church overlooks a little fishing beach frequented by locals from Bakau.

Crocodile Pools

One of three sacred crocodile pools in the country, the locals come to **Katchikali Pool** for the magical properties of its water and healing, ritual baths. Its 6m (20ft) deep 60m (200ft) long pool is said to contain around five large crocodiles.

The other two crocodile pools are at **Folonko**, a long way down the Gambian coast, and **Berending**, across on the north side of the Gambia River estuary.

With a population which just exceeds that of Banjul, Bakau, 'big place' in the local language, is an important stop-off for some people. This town has a good supermarket, **the CFAO**, the Gamtel telecommunications centre, several local markets, shops and a sacred crocodile pool called Katchikali, in the local compound.

There is the main bus stop to the city of Banjul in Bakau, a bank, the Independence Stadium, the Friendship Hotel and the New Town industrial centre. Tourism establishments include the pretty beach-top African Village Hotel in Gambian-style accommodation, with a secluded sea frontage but no real beach, and the Atlantic Village Guest House on a clifftop site above the beach. There is also the Romana Guest House, to the left of the coast road, and all of these offer inexpensive accommodation compared to the larger five-star hotels. Here also is Cham's restaurant, the Chinese Rice Bowl Restaurant on the Old Cape Road, a Lebanese restaurant, the Baalbeck, the Sambou local Restaurant, and the lively Marie's Pub.

Bakau is also the location for many embassy buildings and official residences.

Between Bakau and Fajara beaches, back from the coastal road, is **Kairaba Avenue**, once called Pipeline Road. This leads into Serekunda town and is lined by a few guest houses, the Malawi, Madeline's Inn and the YMCA, two pubs, the Rude Boy Pub and Bobo's Bar, and the Post Office.

(cont'd on page 72)

Fishing

Both The Gambia and Senegal provide the best fishing in all of West Africa. Deep-sea fishing produces record catches; in The Gambia for barracuda, and in Senegal for blue marlin (world record on a 30-pound test line of over 300kg) and sailfish. Senegal is one of the five top locations in the world for sailfish fishing.

The season for billfish is from June to September. Barracuda, king mackerel and kingfish are fished from October to December, and January to March is the season for sea trout and bottom fishing for grouper. April begins the white tuna (bonito) fishing season.

There are around thirty different species of fish to be caught here, either in the Atlantic Ocean, off the beach (shore casting), in the saline estuary, or up-river. These include Hammerhead shark and other shark varieties, tunny, bream, sawfish, swordfish, wahoo, sailfish, barracuda, white tuna, blue marlin, blackfin, skipjack, capitaine, yellowtail, rays, grouper, king mackerel, kingfish, mullet, snapper, tarpon, catfish, rock hind and flying fish. Even giant sunfish have been caught off this coast.

Local fishermen use motorised dugout canoes known as *pirogues* for fishing directly off the beach. These can be hired privately, but organised trips generally use motorised yachts sailing from river mouths and harbours.

Sportsfishing Ltd operates out of the piers at Denton Bridge just outside Banjul, from the shoreline and in the Gambia River or the numerous *bolongs*. It runs half-day barracuda excursions and full-day, all species, trips. Generally there should be a minimum of 4 or 5 fishermen on each trip. Excursions start at 8.00 until 12.00 or 16.00 hours. Meals and refreshments are provided on board and vessels are equipped with VHF radio and often, electronic depth sounders and fish-finders. Other fishing organisations in The Gambia are LA Creek Fishing ☎ 991313, and Il Monda ☎ 466573.

Here also, in **Fajara**, is the West African Tours company office, the Le Lotus Chinese Restaurant, the Two Jays Restaurant and the Bamboo Garden Chinese Restaurant. Opposite this is the Fajara War Cemetery, maintained by the Commonwealth War Graves Commission and containing memorials to those who gave their lives in World War II. On the coast, above the beach, is the Fajara district.

Here, on the left side of the coast road there is Fransisco's small hotel run by a British couple, with Fransisco's Grill House. Also in Fajara is the Presidential residence and the popular Fajara Hotel, with its golf club and 18-hole course.

The Fajara Guest House is on the left side of the road, next to the Fajara Club, a curious mix of English village hall and colonial club with a bar open to non-members. The Novotel and Bungalow Beach complex is on the beach side of the coast road. Facing the beach, on the **Kotu peninsula**, is the Kotu Strand Hotel near the Bakotu Hotel on the **Kotu Stream**.

Not far from here is the Yellow Gate Chinese Restaurant which also serves Malaysian fare. In this area

there are also the Dominoes Bar and the Kotu Bendula Bar in the craft centre next to the Novotel. A little way down south from the well-situated Kombo Beach Hotel is the Badala Park Hotel, across the Kotu Stream from the Kotu Strand Hotel.

Kotu Nature Walk

This area is a favourite of ornithologists, as there are several organised bird-watching and nature walks which can be taken from here. The Kotu Stream attracts a variety of bird life. It is near the Tourist Police HQ and the craft market.

The coast road now runs inland and turns right to follow the coastline to the three-storey Palma Rima Hotel complex with its huge pool, the largest in the country. A few hundred yards from the beach, this hotel also has bungalow accommodation. **Kololi Village**, just a short distance inland, is the location of three guest houses, the Kololi Inn, Kekoi's Happy

Guest House and the Mango Tree Guest House. A little further down the coast and slightly inland is the local village of **Bunkoyo** where nearby is the Bakadaji Restaurant and Hotel.

South of Kotu Point, on the coast, is another fine tourist hotel, the Senegambia, stalwart veteran of the Gambia's tourist trade. Its magnificent gardens and location give the Senegambia the accolade of being one of the best hotels in the country. Inland from the Senegambia Hotel is the popular Uncle Dembo's bar, an excellent craft market and the lovely Dolphin Restaurant. The area is known as Kololi, and there are a few more establishments near the beach like the Di Vino Bar and El Basha Restaurant.

Just three more tourist hotels complete the beachside tourism picture of this part of The Gambia's short coastline. The Kairaba Hotel is now said to be the country's most luxurious and is located on the stunning **Kotu Beach**. The Iberian-style hotel has extensive gardens and there is a craft market and casino nearby. The Holiday Beach Club is located on the same beach as is the Kololi Beach Club, the furthest hotel from Banjul. It is a distance of around 25km (15 miles).

The hotel, however, is the nearest of the beach hotels to Banjul International Airport, 16km (10 miles). Its studio-villa style accommodation faces Kotu Beach and the Bijilo Forest Reserve lies to the south. The Brasserie is a little restaurant located near the forest. Behind the forest are the Boucarabou Hotel, Aji's and the Montrose. South from the forest you will see the headland of Bald Cape.

Beach excursion

From Bijilo Forest, the white sandy beach arcs away to the south, a vast, empty expanse bordered by the white-fringed, blue Atlantic Ocean and the green swaying palms of forest and scrubland. There are a number of settlements along the coastline which runs south, either set on the beaches or inland from the shore, most connected by bush taxi or some form of transport to Serekunda, the big town located inland from the hotel beaches.

Bald Cape is within walking distance of the **Bijilo Forest**

Wrestling is a traditional and national West African sport which the Gambians have developed it into a fine art.

Apart from matches held in the Bakau Stadium, improvised rings are created in town or village outskirts and the competitors strut into the ring to the accompaniment of a local band. They grease themselves in a charmed oil, bind gris-gris amulets and talismans around their arms and legs, and some may have even visited the sacred crocodile pools to gain spiritual and physical strength, a *nyamo*, over their opponents.

Dressed in bright loincloths with a sort of flapping tail, the champions are showered with flowers and gifts from admirers before the bouts start.

A referee's whistle, drowning the drumming and whistling of the musicians, starts the multiple fights. The contestants, usually six at a time, pair up with wrestlers of their own size and the fights begin with a grapple – but these are no holds barred bouts. Biting, kicking and punching, the object is to down your opponent – tourists are advised not to try their luck in the ring!

The bouts generally go on throughout a Saturday or Sunday afternoon and each bout lasts no more than a few minutes. Take a camera with fast film and a handful of loose change for the champions who parade around the ring afterwards, accompanied by a drum troupe, whilst excited tribeswomen abuse the loser.

Another pastime of Mandinka (Mandingo) origin is the warri board, a game as old as the tribe itself. This is best described in the words of an early 17th-century traveller Richard Jobson, who wrote in 1620, *"In the heate of the day they (the Mandingo) passe the time in companies chatting under the*

shady Trees, having one Game with some thirtie stones and holes cut in a piece of Wood, performed by a kind of counting".

Warri is a complex and fascinating game, and *warri* boards can sometimes be found on sale in village markets. Learning the game from a local, is one of the best ways to get to know the people of the Gambia and their customs, but it can be frustrating, and maybe it should be named worry, the correct pronunciation!

Nature Reserve. The forest is a birdwatcher's delight with hornbill, woodpeckers and weavers among the many species to be spotted. A well-marked footpath through the forest takes guided tours on a 5km (3 mile) walk where red colobus and green monkeys, squirrels and large monitor lizards may also be seen. Bijilo Forest contains some of the last remaining rhun palms in the country. From here, the only sounds of life are the flocks of waders, seabirds and the chatter from forest creatures as you stroll along the beach to the cape.

The only signs of life might be the odd temporary shack set up to serve drink to passers-by, or groups of fishermen hauling in their gaily coloured *pirogue* fishing boats. Their catch, which they divide on the beach, might include shark, turtle, tuna, flying fish, yellowtail, sea bream, rock hind, mullet or red snapper.

From Sanimentereng there is a path down to a beautiful white beach. Nearby is the fishing village of **Ghana Town**, named for the number of Ghanaian fish merchants who come here to purchase dried and smoked fish. Next comes

A Holy Site

After Bald Cape you will pass the religious centre of **Sanimentereng** with its mud-built prayer house, ancient baobab tree and sacred pool. Pilgrims come to present gifts at the altar here to gods which are the product of Syncretism, an ancient mixture of pagan and Islamic worship.

a beach used by the fishermen of Brufut village and, from the point, you can see the tiny **Bijilo Islands** and look south down the uninterrupted coastal strand towards more fishing villages.

The promontory of **Salitor Point** is The Gambia's westernmost promontory. Sweeping beaches are interspersed by more headlands like Solifor Point and Sanian Point. It is difficult to round some of these headlands unless the tide is out. It is around 25km (15 miles), as the crow flies, from Salitor Point to the Senegal border. The area around Salitor Point is a popular location for organised beach and bush excursions that can be joined from most hotels.

These full-day safaris include visits to local villages in the interior, a stop at a typical palm-wine tapper's encampment and a midday break for a barbecue on the deserted beach here, which is not far from the fishing village of **Tanji**. It is here that visitors are shown the traditional fish-smoking houses where a fish called the bongafish is cured on wooden racks. A visit to this site, with the long brighty-decorated *pirogue*s drawn up side-by-side on the sand, colourfully-dressed women, or *bananabas*, with baskets of fish on their heads, and hardy fishermen dividing their morning's catch, arranging fish on long drying racks in the curing shed and cooking their lunch in the age-old methods, makes for some wonderful pictures of typical African beach life.

You really need a car or beach buggy to travel any distance further south down The Gambia's short coastline. However, with the right supplies like water, food etc, one can walk the entire coastline from Cape Point, Bakau, to the Senegalese border, a matter of 55km (35 miles). Remember that you will be walking on sand.

There are a series of fishing villages on the way and these include **Tujereng**, with its beautiful Sanyang beach, Sanyang village itself with some fine examples of ancient baobab trees, Gunjur, Bator Sateh and Kartong.

The fishing coast

Gunjur is The Gambia's main fishing village and has a long history of Muslim pilgramage. In the 1800s the town was the centre for a number of Islamic holy men, or *marabouts*, following the visit here of Shekhu Omar Fuitiu. Tribes from miles around used to flock to Gunjur as a place of devotion and learning. There is a tiny mosque on a cliff here which still receives devotees, as do the *marabouts* who have small shrines in their own mud huts.

However, Gunjur is now a commercialised fishing town, a trade which has long eclipsed the town's original attraction of religion and teaching. The Bayo Kunda Campsite here offers accommodation about 2km (1 mile) south of Gunjur town centre.

Kartong is The Gambia's southernmost township and is located on a point overlooking the Allahein (San Pedro) River estuary which is treated as the border between The Gambia and Senegal. A tiny village and police check-point, **Allahein**, is located on the marshy estuary itself. Between the marshy area surrounding Kartong and the coast, the small village of **Folonko** is famous throughout The Gambia.

Folonko pool

Here there is a large sacred crocodile pool which attracts the country's top wrestlers who insist that bathing in the pool increases their prowess in the ring. Certainly the huge Gambian wrestlers might be able to fend off the intentions of the crocodiles, but the barren women who come here to ensure fertility from the sacred waters would be ill-advised to try more than a cupful!

The Folonko Guest House in Kartong should be pre-booked at the British Voluntary Service Overseas office in Banjul.

As The Gambia's coastline is said to be one of the best coastal fishing areas in West Africa, the government is making attempts to streamline the business. However, most folk along the coast fish and cure their catches in the traditional way, although in many cases, the outboard motor has taken the place of paddles and sails. Locals also fish for their own pot as well as supplying the fish freezers of Banjul. The importance of the boat life of the fishermen of this coast is also celebrated in special, lantern-lit processions where boys carry boats made of paper, known as *fanals*, through the village streets.

Fishermen occasionally offer their *pirogue*s for use by tourist hotels which, at night, often organise beach barbecues where traditional dancers are ferried onto the beach by flaming torchlight to entertain the visitors. At Christmas, in many of the hotels, Father Christmas also arrives on the beach in a paddled *pirogue*!

4 THE GAMBIA RIVER – NORTH BANK ROUTE

Crossing by the half-hour ferry trip from Banjul to Barra on the north side of the Gambia River is a trip that almost every visitor to The Gambia makes. This is because one of the country's most famous historic stories has its origins on the north bank. However, there are boat excursions from Banjul which take in this fascinating site. It is also on the itinerary of the North Bank Route which takes the traveller the entire length of The Gambia, following the route of the river almost 640km (400 miles) up-country. Accommodation and eating options, alternative routes and diversions to interesting sites are all indicated.

Above: Descendants of Kunta Kinteh at Juffure

The Slave Trade

The Senegambian region was the hub of the West African slave trade for almost 800 years after Islamic Berbers moved into the region in 1076. Arab Tuareg traders, already long experienced in dealing in 'black ivory', were happy to introduce the first Europeans to arrive in the region, the Portuguese, to their age-old business, slavery. Many indigenous tribal chiefs were also eager to exchange their subordinates for novel Portuguese goods.

In the years subsequent to the opening up of Brazil in 1525, the Portuguese began the first stages of exporting slaves from Senegambia to the Americas. The English were quick to follow the Portuguese. The famous British sea dog, Captain John Hawkins, took the first British consignment of slaves from the Senegambian coast to the colonies of the West Indies in 1562.

By 1570 the French arrived on the coast and began trading salt, iron, firearms and gunpowder for ebony, ivory, gold and slaves. The Dutch West Indies Company established their first slave trading centre on Gorée Island in Senegal in 1617. The Germans also arrived on the scene in 1651 and joined in the lucrative market in slaves.

Roots and Fort James

Travelling independently, take the first ferry crossing in the morning to allow ample time to see the sites. When you reach the jetty of Barra, a taxi should be hired to visit the village of **Juffure**.

The red laterite road leads off to the right of the ferry landing through farmland to Juffure, about 25km (15 miles) inland. Juffure is the location for the story of Alex Haley's book *Roots*, which also made a popular TV mini-series. It was from this small village, or so Haley

Not to be outdone in the slavery game, the Swedes showed up and threw the Dutch off Gorée Island in Senegal in 1655. From then on, European nations squabbled over various slave trading posts for the next 200 years. **James Island**, in the Gambia River estuary, became an important slave-trading station and a collection point for slaves before they were shipped by the British to the Americas. The French, in turn, sent slaves to their West Indian islands, and the Dutch to theirs.

By 1684 there were more than a dozen slave stations operating along the Senegambian coastline and up the two major rivers. Notably these included, in Senegal – St Louis, Gorée Island, Rufisque, Portudal, Jaol, Podor, Matam and Bakel; and in The Gambia – Albreda, James Island, Dog Island and Juffure.

France introduced emancipation towards the end of the 18th century but the French slave trade returned with a vengeance on the orders of Napoleon in 1802. When slavery was abolished by Britain in 1807, they thought fit to establish Bathurst (now Banjul) as a naval port in order to stem the illegal slave trade.

The British Navy captured over 100 slave ships off the Gambian coast in the following few years. It is estimated that around 10 million slaves were shipped from West Africa to the Americas between 1526 and 1810, three million of whom went to Portuguese Brazil.

believes, that his great-great-grandfather, Kunta Kinte, was abducted as a child to be shipped as a slave to the cotton fields of America about 200 years ago.

Juffure village is a typical small cluster of thatched mud-brick huts just a short distance inland from the Gambia River. There are a number of family compounds here, including that of Kunta Kinte and Alex Haley. Visitors are given a short talk on the history of the village and introduced to members of the community including relations of Haley's ancestor.

Above: Early cannon at Albreda

Right: Slave-holding barracks, Albreda

Below left: Fort ruins on James Island

Below right: Up-river boat excursion

One pays small tips to take photographs of one or another of Kinteh's relations and of local village life such as pounding millet.

The British established a trading post here in 1680 and there are the ruins of an older Portuguese trading station, San Domingo, nearby, and a model compound where visitors can see how life went on in the village several centuries ago.

Slave houses and island forts

A short walk towards the river lies the wharf and ancient trading station of **Albreda**, built here by the French slave traders in 1651. It became a French fort temporarily from 1670. Albreda changed hands several times between the English and the French until 1857 when the French left.

An ancient cannon stands near the site, pointing out towards the river.

From Albreda, an hour's ride by dugout canoe takes the visitor to the historic fortress site of **James Island** in the middle of the Gambia River.

The Portuguese had named this Ilha de San Andre (St. Andrew's Island) in the 16th century and traded from an outpost here. In 1651, the base was reconstructed as a fortified trading post by the German Baron of Courland but it fell to French privateers in 1660. It was captured by the British a year later, who named it James Island after the heir to the British throne. They set up the Royal Adventurers of England Trading into Africa company and began business with the Mandinkas trading in gold, ivory, spices, peppers and slaves to be shipped to the West Indies.

'Freedom flagpole'

The crumbling remains of the old slave-holding house still stand at Albreda, but there is no sign of the famous 'Freedom Flagpole'. Whilst the British were here, legend says they set up a flagpole in the compound which, if touched by slaves, would ensure their freedom.

In 1662 the Dutch captured the fort, driving the English onto nearby **Dog Island**, named after the noise made by the baboons found on the island. The British then took the fort again, founding the **British Royal African Company** here in 1684, to be overthrown by the French in 1695. Finally, the British established control on James Island in 1713, only to come under fire from the ships of the Welsh pirate Hywel Davis in 1719.

Six years later, a mysterious explosion in the fort's powder room, blew the fort into the Gambia River. The English rebuilt the fort with stone from Dog Island in 1726 but, when slavery was abolished by the British in 1807, Royal Navy ships used the fort as a base from which to attack foreign slave ships.

The square fort in the middle of the island was abandoned in 1829 to the lizards, snakes and rats which now inhabit it.

Today, the James Island fort is a shell, surrounded by ancient baobab trees, with an entrance arch, battlements, grass-covered ramparts, ruined walls and mute cannon embellished with King George II's Coat of Arms.

'Slave beads'

Parts of the dungeons of the fort on James Island can still be seen, where once up to 140 slaves were held. Visitors often scour the beaches of the island for the blue 'slave beads' which have been found here and were said to have been lost by female slaves incarcerated in the fort, but were probably used for bartering by the Europeans and scattered when the fort blew up in 1725.

Dog Island, rarely visited by tourists, and nearby **Pelican Island**, played an important role in the establishment of Britain's control of The Gambia.

In 1816, Lieutenant Alexander Grant leased Dog Island from the Chief of Kombo for the sum of £75 a year, together with a piece of land on the south side of the Gambia River, on St. Mary's Island, which was to become Banjul. Rock from Dog Island was used to build the first fortifications where Banjul was founded. There is one excursion which takes visitors to Dog Island aboard a

Portuguese-style sailing river craft. Nearby is Pelican Island which has a similar history but is rarely visited on organised excursions.

It was probably from Dog Island that the boundaries of The Gambia were first established in the 1890s. This was done by means of firing a cannon inland from a gunboat stationed off the island, the range of around ten miles being the extent of the boundary between French and British territory. Since then, the boundary has been extended slightly.

Up-river

All the sites of Dog Island, James Island, Albreda and Juffure are located south of the main north road which follows the course of the Gambia River. This road should not be attempted in anything but a four-wheeled drive vehicle as it is mostly unmade and full of pot-holes and obstacles.

Back on this road, out of Barra, the first important settlement reached, north of Juffure, is the village of **Berending**. Here there is one of Gambia's three sacred crocodile pools where pilgrims and wrestlers hope for magical powers from bathing in the waters. The road east is now laterite and dusty, with scrub, thornbush and elephant grass lining the route, and silk cotton trees and baobabs breaking the monotonous horizon.

Occasionally the road dips down to near the Gambia River where creeks or *bolongs* can make the going difficult in the rainy season, although fords and some small bridges span the permanent waterways.

Some of the small hamlets of conical, rondavel-style thatched huts, are clustered around relatively new wells, provided in the 1980s by the Saudi Arabian Islamic Fund. The Muslim religion is endorsed by the presence of small mosques with their minarets striking up through the bush. Makeshift markets along the roadside offer onions, radishes, cassava, yam, brilliant peppers, bananas and oranges for sale, displayed on colourful cloths. Also, mounds of groundnuts, bottles of homemade palm-wine, palm oil and groundnut oil, with paper stoppers, and clay cooking pots are offered on rude tables under a thatched roof.

Stone Circles

Throughout an area including parts of southern Senegal, down across eastern Gambia as far south as Guinea, a collection of ancient megalithic sites still puzzle archaeologists. These are the famed stone circles of West Africa.

They consist of rings up to eight metres in diameter of 10 to 24 rounded, reddish-brown, laterite pillars, from one to two-and-a-half metres in height. Most stones are around a metre in diameter and several tons in weight. The only exception in shape is the 'lyre' or 'V'-shaped stone at Kerr Batch in The Gambia.

There are around 40 such sites in The Gambia, the largest group being at Wassau, and fewer in Senegal. The explorer **Richard Jobson** first discovered the stones in the 1620s. The local legend of a curse on those disturbing the sites added to the enigma of the circles when a series of

expedition leaders including a Captain Doke in 1931, another named Ozanne, and archaeologist Parker, all died in mysterious circumstances after excavating some of the sites.

African tribal leaders hold the sites sacred, but offer no clues as to who built them. Near some circles skeletons, tools, pottery and ornaments have been found, which have been dated to 800 AD. This would place the building of the stone circle to around the time that the great Ghana Empire controlled the Senegambia. However, recent investigations date the stones to 75 AD, indicating that tribes arriving in the region much later than their construction, adopted the circles as burial sites.

A visit to one or more of these sites adds to the magic and mystery of this part of Africa. At the Wassau site, a museum and reception centre have been built, but other sites stand alone in the bleak desert landscape as mute stone testaments to an early, unknown civilisation.

The road passes north of a large town, **Medina Seringe Mass**, where the crossroads is usually a bustle of local traders. Beyond this, the road passes through the villages of Ndungu Kebbe and Kuntair.

A short distance on, a new bridge has now been constructed to replace the ferry over the Jawara Bolong before the large town of **Kerewan**. After Kerewan the road runs through he small settlements of Kinteh Kunda, Saba and Gunjur. Just north of Kinteh Kunda is the town of **Jawara**, once the largest settlement on the north bank of the Gambia River.

After Gunjur, a detour can be made south to break the journey by visiting the town of **Salikene**. This agricultural settlement is based on rice-growing and harvesting fish from the mangrove swamps. A visit here is thoroughly recommended on the journey east as it also provides the opportunity to see some interesting wildlife and bird life in a local setting.

After Salikene, the undulating road leads through more isolated settlements, apart from the township of Nja Kunda, for around 40km (25 miles) over flat agricultural countryside passing No Kunda and Illiassa, the forested area after the Nema crossroads, until arriving at Farafenni.

Farafenni

Farafenni is located around a third of the way along the north bank of the Gambia River and is strategically situated on the main Trans-Gambian Highway.

For this reason it is a large market town, important trucking station and refuelling base and has two hotels. Eddie's Rest House has good accommodation as does the less expensive Fantasia Hotel, south of the town, towards the river ferry 8km (5 miles) south of Farafenni.

On Sundays the big local market or *lumo* is held in the town, attracting people for miles around.

Many visitors do not venture much further up-river, preferring to take the south bank route back to Banjul. This circular route, Barra, the north coast to Farafenni and back along the southern route to Banjul, is a distance of around 325km (200 miles). The Farafenni ferry consists of two flat-bottomed craft, which take all forms of transport, or motorised *pirogues* for foot passengers. The south bank road further up-river is, however, better than the northern route, but the north road offers more in the way of interesting ancient sites.

Forts and stone circles

Continuing east from Farafenni, the route passes through some tiny hamlets like Sukota Fula and Dipa Kunda Wollof, where one can take a detour a short distance north to visit the old fort of **Kantaba**.

It was in the early 1800s that Chief Kemintang organised systematic plundering of British trading ships plying the river up to their base on MacCarthy Island. So successful was his campaign that boat traffic was banned in 1834.

Kemintang extended his territory by recruiting Fula tribesmen and advancing on the small town of Kantaba. The Chief of Kantaba asked the British for assistance and this led to the building of Fort Kantaba in 1842. The resulting battle that year between the British garrison at Kantaba and Chief Kemintang's army, became known as the last of the Badibu Wars. The fort is now in an advanced state of decay.

Returning to the north bank route, the next site to head for is Kaur, passing through the village of **Balangar** on the way. **Kaur** is the site of the nearest of The Gambia's legendary **stone circles** to Banjul. Just outside the village, which has a large

Hippopotamus viewing

Some travellers detour off the main road from the next village of Ngeyen Sanjal to **Sara Kunda**, a large township where a trip down to the Gambia River can be made.

This excursion, which involves a canoe trip from the bank-side jetty at Bambali, gives one the opportunity to see hippopotami, which are endemic in this stretch of the river eastwards. The boat excursion takes the visitor to Elephant Island in the centre of the river.

groundnut collection point, are a number of these mysterious circles of laterite stone pillars out in the dry, dusty grassland. The road here passes several more stone circle sites such as those of up to ten tons at **N'Jai Kunda**, near the town of Njau, and at **Kerr Batch**, famous for its strikingly unusual 'Lyre', or 'V' stone, one of nine pillars.

The road runs close to the winding river and then diverts inland to cross a large creek where a refreshing break can be taken on the banks of the Nainja Bolong before continuing eastwards. There are more stone circle examples at **Kerr Jabel**, a short detour off the road to the south after the Nainija Bolong crossing, and on each side of the road at Niani Maru.

Mysterious Wassau

(See pages 86-87)

The most famous of The Gambia's 'mini-Stonehenge' sites are the numerous stone circles at **Wassau**. These are the largest collection of the phenomenon in The Gambia and indeed, in West Africa. They lie a short distance to the left of the road where a rest house, display room and reception area have been built. Many of these stones weigh several tons and some are up to 2.5m (8 ft) high. The clusters of massive red laterite stones range in number from 10 to 24, in rough circles.

There is a market held at nearby Wassau on Mondays. Just a little further down the road, to the west, is the large town of Kuntaur, located on the north bank of the river.

Apart from the attraction of the stone circles at Wassau, **Kuntaur** is the departure point for visits to the **Baboon Island National Park**, located in the middle of the river a short distance south of the town's ferry stage. Baboon Islands are a group of five forested islands 8km (5 miles) in length, covering 600 hectares (1,500 acres). As one leaves the Kuntaur jetty in a motorised pirogue to visit the islands, the wreck of the riverboat *Lady Denham*, lost in 1929, can be seen protruding from the river waters. It is in this park that the rehabilitated apes raised in the Abuko Wildlife Reserve near Banjul are released into the wild.

Here there are the famous olive baboon and several troupes of chimpanzees.

Berending is a picturesque village on the north bank of the River Gambia, on the way to the Senegal border

Unauthorised parties are not permitted to land. However, a warden might join your pirogue and steer the craft near to where the apes can be photographed. There is the chance, this far up-river, that both hippopotami and crocodiles may be seen in the waters around the islands. The Baboon Islands National Park was founded in 1968. (For visits contact: Ministry of Water Resources, Fisheries, Forestry and Wildlife, 5 Marine Parade, Banjul ☎ 227431.)

After a visit to Baboon Islands, it is not a long drive to the nearest accommodation in Georgetown, on Mac-Carthy Island. However, if you are on a river trip, you will pass Kai Hai Island in the middle of the river before reaching Georgetown.

Back on the north road, the river is joined again at **Lamin Koto** where the Jangjang-Bureh Campsite offers good, but basic accommodation. Opened in 1988, the housing is in typically African rondavel-style huts and there are a restaurant and bar here. This is an excellent base from which to tour the surrounding countryside, take ornithological expeditions or river excursions. The surrounding rice fields are a birdwatcher's delight and there is a single stone circle near here.

Some evenings, the locals from little Lamin Koto village put on traditional dance and music performances for visitors – much more authentic than those seen in the coastal tourist hotels. (For details ☎ 676128, or 495526 in Banjul.)

Man-eating dragon

This is the legendary **Kai Hai Island**. Locals tell of the huge dragon which lives on this densely forested, eerie island; in some tales, it was a vast python with an addiction for local, human meat. There is evidence that a small part of this island was cleared for rice cultivation in the past. It seems as though these attempts have been abandoned – maybe the farmers fell foul of the dragon.

Georgetown

It is a short distance to the ferry to Georgetown. A few minutes on the ferry takes one from the north bank to the **Georgetown** jetty and, as you approach the island, the so-called old slave house building can be seen to the east side of the landing point. The large, stone-bricked building is now a crumbling ruin although the walls look solid enough.

Across the road, the basement of the newish building is said to have been another 'factory' where slaves were held before shipment down-river to be auctioned. More remnants from slavery days can be seen outside the police station, a short walk from the landing stage. Three iron posts which stand outside the police station once offered freedom to those slaves who could reach them.

Georgetown's history goes back to 1823 when the British leased **MacCarthy Island**, or Jangjangbure, as it was then, from King Kolli. Georgetown represents the first attempt by the British at up-river coloni-sation. Two old forts, now in ruins, date from the early 1800s. Certain parts of the town still have the air of an old tropical colonial outpost and some of the old houses, although decaying, are typical of the 1850s.

The Government Rest House is located near the northern ferry terminal, op-posite the police station. The Allah Kabung Lodge and Dreambird Camp is at the end of the town's main street.

Just east of Georgetown is the **Baobolong Camp** with a number of bungalows. You are now around 300km (190 miles) by road from Banjul. MacCarthy Island itself is around 10km (6 miles) long and 2km (1 mile) wide. It is an agricultural island where rice and groundnuts are raised. One of The Gambia's two prisons is located on this island.

On the south side of the island the short stretch of water is navigated by means of a cable-operated ferry.

Should you wish to continue along the northern route to the deeper reaches of The Gambia, return to the Lamin Koto side of the River Gambia and head east. There are several more interesting sites to see on this side of the river.

Above: *Traditional clay oven cookery, Lamin Lodge*
Below left: *Impressive kapok trees dominate the skyline*
Below right: *Termite mounds of this size are common*

Georgetown to Basse

The next leg of the journey east is from Georgetown to Basse Santa Su, commonly known as Basse. This is a bumpy, dusty ride hugging the Senegalese border for a short distance, but you should head for **Karantaba Tenda,** the next important site on this itinerary.

There are two points of interest at Karantaba, the elusive **Monkey Court** and the **Mungo Park Memorial**. The Monkey Court, a natural amphitheatre in the wild, made from a rock formation, is the usual gathering place for a troupe of baboons. The nearest hamlet to this isolated site is either Demba Kali, or way off the main track, Kunting. There may be special tours available to see the baboons from the Jangjangbure Camp near Lamin Koto, back near Georgetown.

At the original site of the old village of Pisania is the concrete memorial obelisk which commemorates the beginning of the final journey of British explorer **Mungo Park**, who twice attempted to find the source of the Niger River in the late 1700s. This site is, however, more easily reached by boat along the river.

In 1795, the 21 year old son of a Scottish farmer from Foulsheils, Selkirkshire, landed at the British slaving port of Juffure, opposite today's Banjul, as part of an expedition. The young Mungo Park (1771-1805) had joined the African Association for Promoting the Discovery of the Inland Parts of Africa in order to find the source of the Niger River and, if possible, be the first white man to visit the elusive city of Timbuctoo.

He had already sailed to Sumatra in the East Indies as a ship's surgeon on *HMS Worcester* (1791-93), but had now decided to explore the eastern route up the Gambia River. He was accompanied on his expedition by a freed Jamaican slave, Johnson, and a local guide named Demba, when his journeys, on horse-back, took him to a place called Kamalia, south of Bamako, in the then Kingdom of Malinke. Here Park succumbed to malaria and was captured by Berber tribesmen who at that time held Timbuctoo, but managed to escape after two months.

Eventually a slave-trader took him back to Pisiana, near

Karantaba Tenda, on the Gambia River, from where he was taken to Fort James and travelled back to England. In 1799, Park published his *Travels in the Interior of Africa*.

The 'Call of the Wild' inspired the now married Park to return to the Gambia on a Government-funded expedition of 45 explorers in 1805. Even before his expedition took off from Pisiana, seven of the party had backed down.

He began his second journey in search of the source of the Niger River with 38 men. Reaching the Niger River Mungo Park managed to send his journal back to Pisiana before being attacked by a local tribe. By that time there were only nine surviving members of the original team of 46.

The entire company was drowned when their canoe overturned, with the loss of all on board. In 1812, seven years later, a slave arrived at Pisiana and told the story of the disaster. In 1815, the account of Mungo Park's last expedition into West Africa was published in London.

The road now heads east across several *bolongs* and flooded creeks and swamps known as *banto faros*. **Darsilami** is one of the larger settlements on the way, just before reaching the tiny hamlet of Yorobawai at the junction of the road leading down to Basse Santa Su.

Basse Santa Su and beyond

After 80km (50 miles) of bad terrain driving, most adventurers will want to take the short detour to the decaying town of Basse, located on the south side of the Gambia River.

Basse Santa Su, The Gambia's easternmost town, consists of a main cotton and groundnut trading point, with a ferry, a school (built in 1929), and a large riverside market held on Thursday mornings. This is the major river-crossing point in the east, used by Gambians and Senegalese alike. Many of the old houses reflect the colonial days of this early 20th century settlement. There is a good assortment of accommodation in Basse, including the Government Rest House, the Appollo 2, the Plaza Rest House, the Agricultural Rest House, the Linguere Motel, the Jem Rest House, and the tiny Basse Rest House.

Finding Roots

Of the millions of Negro slaves shipped from West Africa to work on the sugar and cotton plantations of the New World between the 16th and 19th centuries, few were able to keep any record of their African ancestry. Much of the information about the slaves' African roots was passed on by word of mouth through the generations.

An American called **Alex Haley** endeavoured to trace his ancestry back to the African continent. After exhaustive research in the 1960s and '70s, assisted by the Reader's Digest, he managed to track down a tribal wise man, or *griot*, in The Gambia, who related to Haley the story of a slave trading party who took a small boy from his village many years before.

Piecing together stories related by his black grandmother which told of the abduction of Haley's ancestor in Africa, with the *griot's* tales, and tracing the expedition of a slave-trading party led by a Captain Thomas Davies of England in 1767, Haley tied the three stories together. From details which were mostly fabricated, Haley wrote his successful novel, *Roots*. The book won Haley the **Pulitzer Prize** for literature, and was made into a television series based on the supposed life of his predecessors, from their origins in The Gambia to life as slaves in America, and through to the present time.

Haley had, arguably, identified the birthplace of his ancestor as Juffure, on the northern banks of the Gambia River. His supposedly true story was exposed as a fabrication in 1993. However, today Juffure is a place of pilgrimage for Americans of African descent who believe that their ancestors also lived in this part of Africa before being sold into slavery in the New World.

Irrespective of the fact that Haley's account is myth, it tellingly traces a story which many black Americans can relate to, and Juffure is still welcoming staring visitors to Kunta Kinte's family compound and his string of so-called descendants.

Beyond Basse, this leg of the north-bank journey to the easternmost extreme of The Gambia is similar to that which has already been traversed. However, the ultimate target has to be the **Barrakunda Falls**, on the border between The Gambia and Senegal. Now you are definitely in the Sahel part of Saharan Africa. This is desert country.

It is a tough 64km (40 miles) drive to the next settlement of any import, **Sutukoba**. This was once a flourishing trading town in the late 15th and early 16th century when Portuguese traders came this far, about 480km (300 miles), up-river to meet with trans-Saharan merchants. Its name means Great Sutuko, and Sutukoba, once a town of 4,000, represented the border of the Joloff Empire.

The road rejoins the Gambia River at Fatoto, 24km (15 miles) further on, after passing through the village of Brifu. **Fatoto** is the easternmost ferry crossing point in The Gambia, and a major groundnut collection centre. In this isolated location, with a small market, police station, clinic and

Deep wells

The extreme conditions and lack of water around Sutukoba means that wells must be sunk to great depths to reach water. Gunjur Kuta, a little distance to the north west of Sutukoba, has one hand-dug well 36m (120ft) deep.

Gamtel telephone office, it is good to know that, just 10km (6 miles) south, there is a good road in Senegal with about half an hour of tarmac road to the town and airport of Tambacounda.

A short diversion from Fatoto is the ghost town of **Perai Tenda** with abandoned colonial houses, empty shops open to the Saharan sands, and tumbling grass blowing down empty laterite streets reminiscent of the American Wild West. Further up the river, a dugout canoe trip away, is the easterly border between The Gambia and Senegal, and a few hours further upstream, the Barrakunda Falls lie tantalizingly just over the Senegalese border, near to The Gambia's easternmost point.

5 THE GAMBIA RIVER – SOUTH BANK ROUTE

The south bank road is in much better condition than the route on the north bank of the Gambia River. The journey, initially as far as Basse Santa Su, is 385km (240 mile). Before the real country trek starts, you will have to drive, either from your beachside hotel or from Banjul, through the Kombo area. This includes Serekunda town, passing the Abuko Nature Reserve to the right, Lamin village, and past Banjul International Airport on the left, then into the outskirts of Brikama market town.

At Brikama the road heads east, passing through Kaimbujae Nding, Mandinaba, Pirang, Faraba Banta and Kafuta, all small agricultural villages, going south-east almost to the Senegalese border at Bulok. This road skirts vast areas of mangrove swamp and forest land punctuated by

Above: *A trip up the river amongst the mangroves will be a marvellous experience*

numerous creeks, or *bolongs* which wind into the country from the wide Gambia River to the left. To the right of the road, the scenery is mainly scrubland.

Old trading posts and Kiang West

After the village of Bulok, look out for the sandy track to the left at **Bessi**, which runs north, almost to the riverbank. The site here is known locally as 'Marco', but it is generally called **Brefet** after the old trading post which the British built here in 1664. The French, based in Albreda, on the opposite side of the Gambia River, destroyed the post in 1724, but the British re-built it, only to have it attacked again in 1820. By this time, Britain had abolished slavery some 13 years earlier, and therefore had little use for the outpost. Today it lies in almost indistinguishable ruins, but is worth the 6km (4 mile) detour if searching for historic ruins is your forte.

Continuing east, through the villages of **Somita** and **Sibanor**, you will come to the site of an early Portuguese trading post, **Bintang Gereejal**, where the outlines of a church and the main structure can be traced. A little further east is the town of **Bwiam**, just south of the large winding creek known as Bintang Bolong. **Bintang Bolong** is a favourite cruising waterway for long boat excursions from Denton Bridge in Banjul.

From Bwiam, the straight road passes through Bondali Jola village where there is a campsite called the **Bondali Camp**. The area here is given over to large rice fields. It is

Bwiam

Incongruously, Bwiam has two claims to fame. One is its attractive mosque, and the other is a so-called immovable cooking pot, protruding from the ground in a cotton tree grove just outside the town. This curious, and undated, iron object has been the subject of numerous local tales.

Looking much like an upturned cauldron with a square hole cut in its side, locals call this the *karelo*, or 'cooking pot'. One legend says that this 'pot'

not until one reaches Kalagi village that the road crosses the narrowest part of the Bintang Bolong. A bridge, built in 1962, crosses the *bolong* with a 116m (380 ft) span. Kalagi is also a mustering point for *pirogues,* and some excursion craft from Banjul often moor here.

Turning north, the road heads into the 750km² (290 sq mile) **Kiang West National Park**, which occupies the vast, practically unexplored area between the Gambia River and the Bintang Bolong,

could once swivel to point in the direction of impeding attacks. The object, with its three stumpy 'legs', is certainly immovable but sadly for the romantics, it appears to be no more than the base for some sort of artillery piece, probably cemented into the ground. However, the stories surrounding the 'pot' just illustrate how superstitious and inventive the local people can be!

the longest creek in The Gambia. The Kiang West National Park is the largest of its kind in The Gambia.

At **Sankandi village**, where two British Commissioners were murdered in 1900, the road leading off to the left winds through the Kiang West forest area to **Keneba**, a field station of the Medical Research Council. Even further up this road is a turning to the right which leads to the riverside settlement of Tankular. Tankular was another Portuguese trading post, now abandoned, a short distance from this fishing village which treasures an ancient bell from the post, dating from 1711. Continuing on the main track is the **Kemoto Safari Camp**, also on the Gambia River banks, at Mootah Point. (Details of Kemoto Safari Hotel ☎ 496634.)

Dumbutu to Soma

Continue on the main west-east route, which skirts the border between The Gambia and Senegal, passing **Dumbutu village**, where the British razed a native settlement in 1901 after the Commissioners were killed by the uprising

Above: Nile monitors can reach a metre in length
Left: Tendaba was one of the earliest camps
Right: No bridges cross the wide River Gambia

in nearby Sankandi. The road heads out to **Kwinella village**, site of a fierce battle during the Soniki-Marabout Wars, when around 500 people were slaughtered in 1863. A nearby silk cotton tree grove is the nesting site for hundreds of pelicans.

A road turns off to the left, leading to the popular **Tendaba Safari Camp**. If you want to see yet another ruined trading post, the fortifications and four scattered cannon of the 18th century fortress of **Batelling** can be reached on a short detour from the Tendaba track. Swedish-run Tendaba Camp, 5km (3 miles) from the main road, is located on

The Kapok

This curious West African tree is known variously as the bombax, ceiba, fromager tree (in Senegal), the cotton tree or the kapok. The last two names refer to the cotton-like material that surrounds the seeds of this tree, which hang in distinctive pods from its branches.

This material was once used as a stuffing for pillows, cushions and seats. Local children make a sort of sherbet drink from the dried pods by breaking off the stalk at the top of the shell-like pod, adding water to the seeds and making it into a refreshing drink by stirring the contents with a stick.

Many locals revere the kapok tree as a sacred symbol. They are impressive trees, often growing to a great height with huge

buttress-like roots which form a tangle around the trunk. Kapok trees are often the site of meeting places as the root formation makes ideal back rests while the branches provide shade. Most villages have a veteran kapok which is traditionally the palaver, or discussion place for village elders.

The Senegalese call the kapok, the fromager tree, from the French word for cheese, as its soft, easily chiselled wood inside its yellowish bark, is used to make the dug-out canoes and *pirogues*.

Weaver birds make their nests in this giant kapok

the Gambia River, and was once another trading post. **Tendaba Camp** has a mini-zoo with warthogs, monkeys, crocodiles, antelopes and parrots, and accomodation in rondavel-style huts. (Details of Tendaba Safari Camp ☎ 460608.)

Now the road heads out towards Soma, the main, south bank junction of this road and the Trans-Gambian Highway. Most drivers divert off the main road after Kaiaf to visit **Toniataba**.

Here there is a magnificent thatched great house. The largest example of its kind in The Gambia, this is the traditional house of the local Mandinka Marabout, or holy man and teacher of the Muslim religion, Alhaji Fodali Fati. This old house, known locally as Fatikunda (Fati's House), with its circumference of around 60m (200ft), was the home of an earlier Marabout, Sheik Othman, who was said to have lived for over 100 years and is allegedly buried under the floor. If invited in to see the interior structure of the house, part of which doubles as a mosque, you should remove your shoes.

Soma town has a large market and is a major trans-continental trucking station. Ensure you have sufficient fuel for any onward journey before leaving the bustling hubbub of Soma. The Traveller's Lodge in Soma offers accommodation. The alternatives here can mean driving north to the ferry crossing over the Gambia River to Farafenni and the north bank route, or continuing on eastwards up-country.

Soma to Basse

Near Soma is the small, quiet township of **Mansa Kongo**, or the King's Hill. This is the district's administrative centre.

The scenery from here-on changes dramatically. Mangrove swamplands give way to proper African bush and jungle forest. The road passes through **Jappeni** and then through a large expanse of deep forest.

North is the river with Elephant Island located in mid-stream. Elephant Island can only be reached from the jetty on the north coast settlement of Bambali. It is from Elephant Island that the river becomes the habitat of hippopotami.

The Mangrove

When John Steinbeck wrote "No-one likes the mangrove," he was voicing an opinion which could be echoed around the tropics. With the tree's tangle of roots buried deep in stinking mud, its ungainly branches and shiny, leathery leaves, the mangrove, or mangle, can in no way be called graceful or attractive. However, the great expanses of mangrove swamp which line the West African coastline conceal an entire ecosystem upon which the very balance of nature depends.

The mangrove is a tropical evergreen which thrives in salty, tidal mudflats spurned by other plant life.

There are three main varieties of mangrove; the **white** mangrove prefers a muddy soil, the **black** variety a marshy habitat on the upper tidal zone, and the **red**, with its characteristic branching root system, grows between the high and low water marks. Each is salt-loving and they are among the few plants which can cope with water of a high salinity. However, the mangrove also enjoys a climate which has a high humidity and prefers regions with a high rainfall.

The trees of the red mangrove grow in clumps between the low and high tidal watermarks and can reach 24m (80ft) in height. This variety is immediately recognised by its tangle of roots protruding from the central trunk and embedded in the water or mud. These prop roots take oxygen from the air. Around the base of the black mangrove trunk, aerial roots known as pneumatophores strike up like grass, and also absorb oxygen from the air. The mud in which the red mangrove buries its roots is

(cont'd on page 107)

The route now strikes north through vast rice fields to the village of **Pakaliba**, where there is the Sofanyama Camp Site. This is located just before Pakaliba village itself, on the pretty **Sofanyama Bolong**, sheltered to one side by a rocky bluff standing proud of the flat countryside. A small bridge crosses the Sofanyama Bolong. (For details of Sofinyama Camp Site ☎ 49526.)

The croc hunter's tale

There is a myth in Pakaliba of a local crocodile hunter, Bambo Bojang, who was attacked by the crocodiles he was stalking, but avoided being eaten by a mystic power. His name is now legend in the region and his story is related in a long local song.

The next stop, **Jarreng**, is a market village specialising in cane and rafia furniture and some wonderful ceramic work. If you are on an organised tour, the guide might suggest buying kola nuts to give to the

The Mangrove

(cont'd from page 105)

created from the large quantity of dead vegetation and detritus which the tree produces and which rots down into a particularly nutritious, rich mire. So much vegetation-based mud is created that the red mangrove literally creates land, leapfrogging with its roots to further banks of litter as new banks of mud are created. The red mangrove creates almost three tons of leaf litter per acre per year.

Red mangrove flowers with large, fleshy, yellow blossoms and the tree's quill-like seeds germinate whilst still on the tree. A tree produces around 300 seeds per year and a seedling grows to between 18 and 36cm (7 to 14in) long before they detach themselves from the branch. When the seeds finally fall into the surrounding water they gradually invert to a vertical position because of their in-built buoyancy pouch and drift easily with the current.

Upon reaching land or mud, the seeds quickly grow, attaining 60cm (2ft)in the first year, although seeds can drift alive for up to a year. Those seeds which fall onto the soft mudbanks embed themselves into the mire like daggers. In the second year, the new mangrove puts out prop roots. In this way the mangrove quickly colonises new land.

As the tree grows, a rich mixture of sediment builds up trapped in the network of prop roots. This attracts a profusion of wildlife which is interdependent and relies on the mangrove for a variety of essentials. Spiders and mosquitoes, sandflies, wasps and dragonflies find the mangrove swamps an ideal habitat and, in turn, provide food for larger life like ghekos, anole, lizards and iguanas. Tree snails thrive on the rotting vegetation. Apart from sea-

(cont'd on page 109)

Opposite top: *'Slave market' at Georgetown*

Opposite bottom: *Cane seats are more comfortable and durable than they look*

locals in return for the chance of visiting a traditional compound. Nearby is a ferry point from which canoes can take visitors to the 15km (9 mile) long Papa Island in the Gambia River. A dog-leg in the road takes the visitor through Sotokoi to **Kudang**, from which a detour can be made to visit the huge groundnut collection station at Kudang Tenda on the Gambia River, opposite Pasari and Deer Islands.

It is now a long, 50km (30 mile) drive to MacCarthy Island and the important centre of Georgetown. Just before turning north to meet the hand-operated cable ferry across the Gambia River to MacCarthy Island, there is a monument to look out for. This monument was erected on the left hand side of the road to commemorate the efforts of the Chinese who worked on the National Rice Project here in the 1950s and '60s. Should you wish to stop over in Georgetown you will have to turn off the main south bank route to Sankuli Kunda and the ferry terminal.

However, continuing east on the south bank road, the countryside becomes wilder and hilly. At **Bansang** there is

the second of the country's two main hospitals, the other being in Banjul. There is a ferry at Bansang, and one can cross the river here to join the north bank route. The region here is famous for its pottery, silverwork and excellent river views. Look for the particularly attractive incised and painted clay pots made in Sotuma and Aldhungari. These can also be purchased in the market at Basse Santa Su, the next stop on the route. The Bunyada Hotel offers accommodation in Bansang.

On ariving in Basse Santa Su, commonly known as Basse, the road east now turns into a dirt track which runs through the townships of Fatoto. The road east of Fatoto, to Koina, almost on the easternmost border between The Gambia and Senegal, is even worse. The only place of any note on this leg of the journey is **Kristi Kunda**, or Christ's Home, once a missionary post and school, lying a short distance east of Fatoto. The road deteriorates even more now, but if you are determined to reach the easternmost border and Barrakunda Falls on this route, head for the village of Koina, after which there is a 15km (9 mile) trek.

The Mangrove

(cont'd from page 107)

grass and littoral plants which may take root around the mangrove, shrimps, crabs and fish seek shelter and food in the network of roots. *Nudibranchs* or sea-slugs thrive on the minute algae which build up around the mangrove roots and oysters such as *Crassostrea* and *Isognomon*, and mussels cling to the lower parts of the roots, as do sponges and anemones. Starfish, sea urchins and jellyfish find nutrients in the rising and falling waters around the mangrove roots. Great colonies of fiddler crabs live in burrows in the higher parts of the mudbanks, feeding off dead animal remains, small shrimps, and sifting the mud for food.

In the deeper waters of the mangrove swamps, yellowtail snappers, eels, catfish, bass, snook, tarpon and lobsters can be found. Crocodiles seek shelter and food in the labyrinthine channels between mudbanks. Wildfowl, herons and egrets roost in the high branches, all contributing to the richness of the land which the mangrove is creating.

Man fishes the waters of the mangrove swamps and harvests mussels and oysters from its roots. The hard, close-grained red-coloured wood is used for firewood, in charcoal-making, as building material and carves well. The mangrove acts as a buffer-zone between land which could easily be eroded by the sea, and the tides. It also acts as a filter by breaking down a certain amount of waste which would otherwise pollute the shoreline. Also, as the red mangrove encroaches on the sea, creating new land, and the black, white and buttonwood varieties follow, the land left behind can either be cultivated or is populated by new terrestrial vegetation.

The mangrove may, as Steinbeck wrote, be unloved, but it has its many uses.

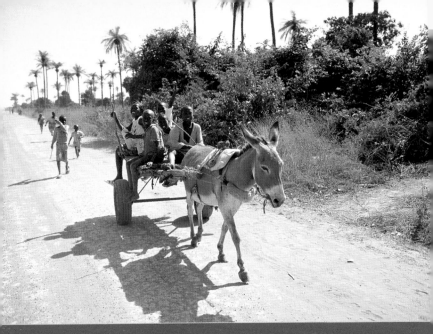

6 SENEGAL

WELCOME TO SENEGAL

Visitors to The Gambia rarely venture across the border into the vast country of Senegal which surrounds Africa's smallest nation. However, there are organised tours from The Gambia which give tourists an insight into French-speaking West Africa. The contrasts experienced between the two countries makes a visit into Senegal a rewarding add-on to either a package holiday or more specialised trip. Those visitors driving up-country in The Gambia or venturing to the extremes of its coastline, might feel tempted to cross the border to discover a land which offers 'real' Africa on a much larger and more exotic scale than its tiny neighbour.

Above: Children with a donkey cart in the bush

Senegal – a land of superlatives

It is West Africa's flattest country and the River Senegal, after which the country is named and which forms much of its border, is one of Africa's longest rivers. The Niokolo-Koba National Park, West Africa's best game reserve, is home to Africa's largest breed of lion. Senegal has Africa's longest running democracy, but it also has West Africa's largest National Debt. Senegal was the first West African country to be inhabited, the first 'black' African country to be explored by Europeans, the location of the first railway in the region, and it is now the biggest West African holiday destination.

Senegal really deserves an entire guidebook to itself but, since many visitors to The Gambia like to make excursions into this part of Francophone Africa, a short account of the country is considered essential.

Vibrant Dakar, with its own special culture and its internationally renowned music and dance, is a great tourist draw, as is the wild African big game of the country's three reserves such as the Niokolo Koba National Park. Many foreign visitors to The Gambia also stray across the practically unmarked border into the Casamance region of Senegal in the south. Here they can experience a vastly different lifestyle from that in The Gambia.

Senegal's fascinating past also attracts visitors to ancient sites like the Senegambian stone circles, Gorée Island and St. Louis. Others find the French-African way of beach life a contrast to that in English-speaking Gambia, and gravitate to the fine beaches of the Cape Vert peninsula or those of the Little Coast.

The Senegal people too, varying from dark-skinned Berber traders in flowing robes, to the haughty Wolof, present the visitor with contrasting cultures and customs. Senegal is strikingly different from The Gambia and even a day's excursion into the country can be a revealing insight into this part of Africa and enhance your visit to The Gambia.

A Geographical Outline

Senegal is the nearest tropical country to Europe. Bordered to the north and east by the long Senegal River, France's first West African colony embraces the country of The Gambia much as the profile of a head surrounds the mouth. Around its borders, Senegal's neighbours include Mauritania, Mali, Guinea and Guinea-Bissau. The majority of the country is dry and sandy with the wettest part being the Casamance region, just south of The Gambia. Much larger than the tiny enclave of Gambia, Senegal covers almost 200,000 km^2 (76,000 sq miles), around the size of Britain.

The 480km (350 miles) of Atlantic coastline lie mostly to the north of the Gambia River with the delta region of the Casamance River forming the shorter southern coast. The nose of the 'head profile' outline of the country is the volcanic peninsula of Cape Vert, the westernmost point of the continent. This protects the city and port of Dakar, the capital. Inland, the countryside is mostly flat and semi-desert with some hilly country in the south-east.

People and Culture

The name Senegal comes from the Zenaga Berbers who invaded the country from Mauritania during the 11th century. In the northern part of Senegal the majority of the population are still of Berber stock, Arabic in origin. The Berbers brought Islam to the region which is now predominantly Muslim.

As with The Gambia, Senegal is an Islamic country with a great diversity of tribes comprising the population of around 7 million, 80 per cent of which are Muslim whilst the rest are either Christian or Animists. The larger part of the country is peopled by negroid tribes, mostly Mandingo. Of these, the majority are of the Wolof group, followed by the Serers,

Toucouleurs, Diolas, Fulani and Malinke.

Politics and the Economy

Senegal achieved independence within the French Community in 1960. It has an elected President who serves for a five-year term and appoints a Prime Minister and a 28-strong cabinet. The legislative National Assembly consists of 120 members.

The production of groundnuts and the country's fishing industry combine to create Senegal's main exports apart from a small trade in phosphates. The country has more African fishermen than any other country on the continent. More than three-quarters of the country is occupied by agricultural production. Cereals like rice, millet, maize and sorghum are the main crops, as well as sugar cane, tomatoes, other vegetables and cotton. Livestock, particularly cattle, are raised throughout the country. Dakar is a major port and the shipbuilding industry is an important business, as are the manufacturing of textiles and food-processing. France is Senegal's main trading partner with the UK coming second due to the large demand for groundnut oil and phosphates.

Top Tips

Some of Senegal's major attractions are tantalisingly near to The Gambia, therefore the country's major points of interest are detailed. Few visitors to The Gambia will be able to afford much time for an excursion into Senegal; however, there are several options for a day or two's visit.

In this listing the symbol [*] indicates historic monuments; the symbol [**] indicates local life; and the symbol [***] indicates bird and wildlife.

Dakar and Gorée [*]

Dakar, six hours drive from Banjul, and the capital of Senegal, is a modern, bustling city with skyscrapers dwarfing old houses, mosques and museums. The numerous markets of Dakar attract tribesmen in colourful costumes from way up-country. In contrast, Gorée Island is quiet and peaceful, which belies its past as a slave centre. Many historic monuments still stand from that time, protected by UNESCO.

St. Louis [*]

This northern city, West Africa's oldest, is centred around a long island between the Senegal River and the Atlantic Ocean. Its marvellous old colonial houses protected by UNESCO, its early church, fort and grand palace are among many attractions.

Sine Saloum [***]

This area is within a day's outing from The Gambia and

is a birdwatcher's paradise, with many migratory and endemic birds, local fishing villages and numerous coastal waterways. This is a National Park.

Casamance [**]

The region south of The Gambia, reached easily within a day's excursion, offers untouched African estuarine delta life where villages survive on fishing and growing rice. The wildlife is prolific in its many waterways, *bolongs* and creeks surrounding the Casamance River delta. French-speaking fishing folk live in traditional thatched villages, some on stilts, evoking an 'African Camargue' environment.

Niokolo Koba [***]

For the big game synonymous with African life. The National Game Park lies a good two-day's journey from the Gambian coast. Elephant and lion may be seen from the safari lodges in this protected forest area. Up-river travellers often cross the border into Senegal to visit Tambacounda and take an onward journey to the national park. An overnight stay or two is recommended.

This traditional head-dress is a 'tiko' in Mandinka

Above: *Gaily decorated bush-taxis*

Below: *The Oil Palm yields cooking oil and palm wine*

A SNAPSHOT OF SENEGAL

Dakar

Senegal's capital city is built on a promontory, Cap Vert, which is the most westerly point in Africa. Although it was not established until 1857, it is the oldest European city in West Africa. Visitors from The Gambia will usually arrive in this city of nearly a million people by road.

The autoroute takes the visitor through the suburban town of **Rufisque**, past Yof International Airport to your right, and directly into the bustling centre of the city. The cultural shock of coming from the barren wilderness of the country drive to meet head-on the loud, brash, high-rise, modern hubbub of Dakar's city life, can be staggering. Comparing Dakar with Banjul is like comparing a sleepy English village with New York, and the language and currency are different, French and the CFA.

Depending on how long you are staying, accommodation would be the first priority. There is a wide range of hotels in Dakar, from the very cheap to the height of luxury, although all accommodation in the city is comparatively expensive and there is a small tourist tax on all hotel rooms. It can take three days properly to see the sights in and around Dakar.

From the imposing green-tiled, white-painted, 1907 **Presidential Palace** on the Corniche to the south-east of the city centre, it is a short walk down the Boulevard de la Republique to the city's massive **Cathedral du Souvenir Africain**, with its Byzantine-like cupola. The cathedral is almost on the large roundabout of the Place Washington where you will find the **Theatre Daniel Sorano**.

A couple of blocks south from here is the Dakar Museum. Known as the **IFAN Museum**, this contains a collection of early African masks and costumes, statues and furniture, plus displays of African musical instruments and agricultural tools.

Up Avenue Jean Jaures from the Place Washington, you will find the Ministry of Tourism to the left, on Avenue A. Peytavin. Turn right, along Avenue Pompidou and, a couple of blocks on the left, is one of Dakar's most colourful attractions, the lively **Sandaga Market**.

Market visits

These are an essential ingredient of any visit to Dakar – there are several markets in this part of the city where you can buy just about everything, the **Kermel** and the **Tilene** being among the largest. Buy silver and gold jewellery, wood carvings, pottery, embroidery, wickerwork and artworks.

From the Marche Sandaga up the Avenue Emile Badiane, the Sand Painter's Yard and artworks of Keur Jean Thiam (in the old Mauritanian silversmith's yard, the Cour des Orfevres) are well worth seeing. Continuing up this street, you will come to the **Medina Quarter** of the city and the 70m (230ft) minarets of the **Grande Mosque**, completed in 1964. Every day, except Friday, you can climb a minaret, giving fantastic views of the city and its location, surrounded by the deep blue of the Atlantic Ocean.

From the Mosque, take Avenue Faidherbe east, down to the ornate Railway Station. From here you can walk south, past the Place de l'Independance, back to the Presidential Palace and its guards in their fezzes. There is no shortage of places to eat at bar and music venues in Dakar. For a bit of peace and quiet, you can take a taxi out to the beaches of Yof and Ngor, beyond the airport.

One of Dakar's major attractions is not in the city at all. Directly east from the Corniche Est, behind the Presidential Mansion, the tiny Island of **Gorée** has an international reputation and a poignant history. The island itself, just under a kilometre in length (half a mile), requires a half-day excursion from Dakar. Most visitors find Gorée Island more fascinating than Dakar city itself.

Ile de Gorée

When the Portuguese first arrived in West Africa in

Gory Gorée

Of the many slave houses still preserved along the West African coastline, that on the Isle of Gorée, near Dakar, remains the most poignant. Symbol of all that was inhumane in the trading of slaves from Africa to the Americas, the old slave house, built by the Dutch in 1676, vividly brings the tragedy to mind.

Shackles, slit windows and dark chambers measuring 6m (20ft) by 10m (33ft) where the terrified slaves were crammed, inspected, priced, branded and then shipped to the slave auctions in the New World, now form part of its museum. Between capture and shipping, many slaves died and were tossed to the sharks. Obstinate slaves were shackled to the walls in pens which would half flood with seawater at high tide.

There were a number of these slave houses on the Island of Gorée. Just one remains today, with a twin, curved entrance stairway leading to the slave masters' quarters above the holding pens.

The French took Gorée island from the Dutch in 1677, and it changed hands several times after that as a slave trading base for Europeans. The British abolished slavery in 1807, but the French continued trading in 'black ivory' until the 1820s.

In 1816, the French Brigantine *Medusa* sailing towards Gorée with Senegal's new governor plus 400 crew and soldiers, foundered off the West African coast. Shipwrecked survivors took to an improvised raft and were rescued after weeks adrift. Just 15 people survived the tragedy, thought by some to be an act of divine retribution. The sufferings of the 150 people who took to the *Medusa's* raft inspired the French painter, Jean-Louis Andre Gericault, to paint his enormous canvas, the *Radeau de la Meduse* or *The Raft of the Medusa,* between 1818-19.

1444, they landed on Gorée, naming it Palma. In 1482 the Portuguese built a church here on the site which is now occupied by the island's oldest structure, the 17th century Police Station. The Portuguese began a slave-trading business based on the island, which was to continue for the next 400 years. The Dutch gave the island its present name in 1588, by calling it Goede Reede, or Good Harbour.

France took the island as a trading base in 1677. Colonising the island with traders, the social structure of Gorée developed a unique and powerful matriarchal hierarchy formed by French wives, daughters and female slaves. This was known as the age of the *sigares*. Before Dakar was established in 1857 as an overspill from Gorée, the population of the island numbered over 5,000.

To the south of the island there are the ruins of successions of forts, now known as **Le Castel**. To the north is the **Fort d'Estrees**, housing the IFAN Historical Museum with displays tracing the country's history. Apart from the single Slave House still standing on the island, there are numerous beautiful, but dilapidated colonial houses and official buildings. A fine example is the **House of Victoria Alberis**, now the Historical Museum. One of the country's oldest mosques, made of stone, still stands on the island.

In 1970 UNESCO declared the island a site of World Heritage. See the **Museum of the Sea** with some fascinating exhibits. There are no cars or bicycles, and only 1,000 people on Gorée. The peace and calm of Gorée belies its grim slave-trading history.

Iles des Madeleines

Naturalists might take a diversion from Dakar to visit the Iles des Madeleines, a National Park and botanical and bird sanctuary. Interesting specimens include the Dwarf Baobab and the Tropic Bird, found only here.

St Louis

Some visitors to Dakar make the 268km (171 mile) journey by train or road, north, to the historic city of St Louis. The oldest French settlement in Senegal it was founded by Louis Caullier in 1659. Senegal's third largest city with a population of 100,000, it is the regional capital, located almost on the border of Mauritania in Northern Senegal. Until 1958 St Louis was the capital of both Senegal and Mauritania. Like Gorée Island, it is a UNESCO site of World Heritage.

St Louis' main attractions are on the long, narrow island which stands in the middle of the Senegal River, between the mainland and a spit of land dividing the river from the Atlantic Ocean. The island is reached by one of two bridges, the larger is the **Faidherbe Bridge**, transferred here from its Danube location in 1897. Across this bridge is the **Governor's Palace**, once a fort during the 17th century.

The **cathedral**, Senegal's oldest surviving church, near the Palace, was built in 1828. The island's beautiful 18th and 19th century European-style colonial houses and old trading houses, with balconies, verandas, wrought iron work and fenestrations, and their inner courtyards are a delight, even though most are in a state of decay.

The **Maison des Signares** on Quai Henry Jay, named after the half-caste females who enjoyed a matriarchal hierarchy in the 18th and 19th centuries, is typical of the St Louisienne architectural style. This is located near the island's **Museum**, which traces the history of the region from Neolithic times to the present day. Many of the island's streets were laid out in 1873 and named after famous French writers.

World champion

St Louis' more recent claim to fame was Battling Siki, the first and only African heavyweight boxing champion of the world in 1925. Born M'Barick Fall, in St Louis, he was assassinated the same year in America.

Across one of the two bridges which link the island with the spit, the area to the north has some gracious old colonial houses, and is called **Ndar Tout**. To the south, on the spit, is a typical fishing quarter and unusual fishermen's graveyard.

Two national parks

North of St Louis, you can drive up to two National Parks. These are rather off the beaten track, but are important to wildlife enthusiasts. Driving to the **Langue de Barbarie National Park** and the **National Bird Reserve of Djoudj**, is by four-wheeled drive vehicles and is really for the adventurous. Flamingos, pelicans, turtles and crowned cranes can be seen in both parks in abundance.

The **Parc National des Oiseaux du Djoudj** boasts around 100,000 flamingos and 10,000 white pelicans, making it the third largest concentration of these birds in the world. Between October and April the pelearic bird population musters here, near the Mauritanian border.

Accommodation in the Parks is good but expensive.

Senegal, up-river

Few short-time visitors to The Gambia will have enough time or the opportunity to travel far inland in Senegal. However, for those that do, there is a completely different side to the country from that of the coast, up-river.

The centre of Senegal is relatively empty and barren, its sandy plains dotted with kapok and baobab trees and little else. A few nomadic herders live in this wilderness which becomes more like the Sahara the further north or east one travels. This is known as the **Ferlo** but, forming the national boundaries between Senegal and Mauritania to the north, and Mali in the east, the long Senegal River provides a fertile plain which is heavily populated in places. Almost 1,800km (1,110 miles) in length, the River Senegal rises in Guinea, to the south of the country, and flows in a great arc around Senegal.

The city of St Louis, on the Atlantic coast, was founded at the point where the Senegal River flows out into the ocean. The river is tidal for the last 500km (300 miles) but large ships can only

The 'Upside Down' Tree

The baobab is West Africa's most distinctive tree. Although it does not grow to the height of its cousin, the kapok, which can reach 50m (160ft), the baobab can grow to 21m (70ft). It is the tree's weird shape that makes it stand out from other vegetation. The grotesque trunk can reach 9m (30ft) in girth and, from all angles of the trunk, gaunt ungainly branches protrude like roots. The local legend suggests that this tree was uprooted by the devil and plunged, upside down into the earth.

Traditionally, the Africans endow the baobab with magical properties, not only because of its ability to store water but because the powdered leaves, *alo*, are used to cure rheumatic ailments and inflammations, and the pulp of the acidic yellow fruit is known as a remedy for circulatory problems. The pulpy nature of the baobab fruit has given it the local name of 'monkey bread tree'.

Most villages have a sacred baobab tree which, unlike any other tree, after a certain age gradually gets shorter. Many of these village trees are said to be over 1,000 years old.

There are many uses for the parts of the baobab apart from those for its fruit. The bark is said to have anti-malarial qualities and the phosphate-rich seeds are

used to make soap and fertilizers. The bark is carved to make musical instruments, and rope, cloth and packing material is also made from the bark. When dead, the spongy wood of the trunk is hollowed to make fishing boats, giving the tree the name of 'cork tree'. Very old baobab trees generally lose the centre of their trunks and these hollow trees have been used as temporary accommodation by wandering nomads. A more permanent use of the hollow trunk in olden times was as a living coffin in which *girots* of the minstrel class were interred.

Above: Did the devil re-plant this ancient Baobab upside down?

navigate as far as Podor, 280km (180 miles) up-river. It is from St Louis that one begins the journey up the Senegal River, which can be done either by road or preferably, by river ferry boat.

The wide estuary of the river has created a vast, long spit of land between the Atlantic Ocean and the mainland on which St Louis is built but, south of the river, between its bank and the vast **Lac de Guiers**, is Senegal's third largest National Park.

Travelling further up river, through a large rice and sugar cane producing area, the town of **Rosso** is the main border site for the cross-over into Mauritania. A ferry takes passengers and vehicles across the river which forms the national border. There is little to see here in Rosso. For a little bit of history one has to travel a short way further up-river to **Richard Toll**.

Founded in the 1820s by a rich French planter named Claude Richard, Richard Toll means 'Richard's Field'. In the middle of a tributary of the Senegal River is an island where a Baron Jaques Roger built his mansion and botanical park. The remains of this grand colonial mansion, built by the Governor of Senegal (1822-27), still stand, surrounded by trees imported from France, cocoa palms and date groves. There are plans to convert this building into an hotel.

The Parc National des Oiseaux du Djoudj

This lies 60 km (40 miles) from St Louis, and is also rated as the third most important bird reserve in the world with more than 3 million birds here at any one time. Some of the world's largest concentrations of white pelican and pink greater flamingo, amongst a wealth of other bird life, are found in this 60,000 hectare (150,000 acre) park, which is now a UNESCO World Heritage site.

Podor and beyond

Just 24km (15 miles) further upstream, past a vast dam, is the fortress and town of **Dagana** and one of the largest inland islands in West Africa has been formed by the Senegal River. **Podor**, one of Senegal's oldest cities, inhabited since the third century, is located on the northernmost tip of the marshy, 80km (50 mile) long, **Ile a Morphyl**. The British built a fort here in 1745, and the French reconstruction of this can still be seen. There is *Campement* accommodation in Podor.

From Podor, it is a long 220km (140 miles) upstream to the next settlement of any importance. The town of **Matam**, noted for its jewellery and pottery crafts-manship, is the site of Louis Faidherbe's earliest colonial fortress, still standing on the banks of the river as it has since 1847, together with an old colonial mansion known as the Residence de Djourbivol. The mosque at Matam is a particularly attractive piece of architecture, dominated by two tall minarets. Although there is no hotel here, one can always find a room.

Elephants' Graveyard

Legend tells of a vast herd of elephants which were marooned on the Ile a Morphyl (Island of Ivory), and which died out centuries ago, giving rise to the tale of the long-lost Elephants' Graveyard.

At **Bakel**, even further up the Senegal River, are the impressive remains of another of Faidherbe's forts, the third most important in Senegal, and now occupied by the Prefect of Bakel and not open to the public. Even before the 1847 fort was constructed, the explorer Rene Caille built himself a grand pavilion in Bakel in 1819. This red-roofed, church-like structure is still well preserved and dominates the fort and the river below, an incongruous structure in this lonely, isolated outpost lying 500km (315 miles) inland from the coast. The Hotel El Islam or Hotel de Boudon offers accommodation in Bakel.

Above: Senegal and The Gambia have four crocodile varieties. This is the Nile crocodile

Left: The common Vervet monkey is a member of the Green monkey family

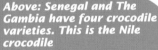

The furthest town up the Senegal River, lying on the border with Mali, is **Kidira**, 640km (400 miles) upstream from St Louis. There is no hotel or accommodation here, and few adventurers make the journey this far. However, Kidira stands on the Dakar to

Bamako (Mali) railway line and is a major market centre. Both the rail line and a road lead directly west from Kidira to the large town of Tambacounda, a journey of 200km (120 miles).

Tambacounda is just a short distance east of the border with The Gambia. This is a major confluence of trading routes both from Mali, Guinea, Dakar and The Gambia. There are a number of places to stay or eat here and a vast market. There is a good road from Tambacounda, via Velingara in Senegal, to Basse Santa Su in The Gambia.

The Sine-Saloum

A day's excursion from Banjul might include a visit to the Mandinka Village of **Missira**, a *pirogue bolong* boat ride to visit **Sifo Island** and its local fishing village in territory abounding with bird life, and visiting the Keur Saloum Hotel on the nearby creek.

There are a number of similar excursions which can be made easily into this fascinating region which is a National Wildlife Reserve. This area is almost twice the

size of The Gambia but the most visited part is the **Saloum delta**, the nearest part of Senegal to Banjul. The River Saloum is the third largest in Senegal. This is one of the most attractive regions in Senegal, with creeks, islands, rice fields, hardwood forests, and a long Atlantic coast of dunes and sandy islands.

Kaolack is the regional capital of the Sine-Saloum and the centre of the country's groundnut business. Attractions here include the second-largest covered market in Africa, and the **Tidjani Mosque**. However Kaolack lies inland from the delta and is not generally visited by travellers from The Gambia unless on the way to Dakar. **Toubacouta**, the nearest town to The Gambia, lies on the banks of the delta and is generally visited on the way to an excursion from the village of Missira. The National Park's headquarters are just 6km (4 miles) from Missira.

Wildlife here ranges from fiddler crabs and mud skippers, to schools of dolphins and crocodile. Naturally, fishing is excellent here and the local delicacy is oyster, harvested from the exposed roots of

Exotic bird life

Excursions into the Saloum delta are a must for birdwatchers, camera and binoculars essential, as are some warm and waterproof clothing for *pirogue* trips. A tour in a *pirogue*, out into the maze of waterways, swamps and lush estuarine vegetation, will reveal a multitude of bird life, especially during the migratory season, November to April. Flamingos, pelicans, rosy spoonbills, spur-winged geese, storks and waders, flock to the shallow mudflats. Osprey, buzzards, Cape cormorants, black-crowned night heron, hammerkop, pied kingfisher, wildfowl and egrets patrol the mangrove regions, and the palm plantations are ideal habitat for golden bishops, orange-cheeked waxbills, bee-eaters, rollers, weavers, hornbill, sunbirds, the Senegal coucal and violet starlings.

Large birds like the palm nut vulture, the West African harrier, Verreaux's eagle owl, and the rare long-crested hawk eagle might also be seen.

the mangrove trees. There are manatee, or dugongs, in the saline waters, and hippopotami have sometimes been sighted. On land, river hogs, warthogs, small deer, green, vervet, red colobus and patas monkeys are found, as well as tribes of baboons and some fair-sized python.

Numerous safari camps, *campements*, and hotels have been built in the region for foreign visitors and they range from the inexpensive, like the locally-owned Hotel le Caiman at Sokone, west of Kaolack, to the excellently-located but rather expensive Le Pelican, at Ndangane in the north of the region.

North of the Sine-Saloum delta and National Park, a long, straight stretch of coastline offers some wonderful sandy beaches running north, almost to Dakar city itself. This is known as the **Little Coast**, and is Senegal's second best beach area. The road from The Gambia to Dakar, after sweeping around the

Saloum delta, joins the Little Coast at M'Bour, halfway up this shoreline.

The Casamance region

South of The Gambia is a vast delta known as the Casamance, after the large river. Again this region is a birdwatcher's wonderland, attracting millions of migratory birds which bring ornithologists from across the globe to see some of the rare and beautiful species which flock here.

Not only do great numbers of birds migrate here but, until a recent political disturbance which has now died down, many hundreds of tourists, mainly French, flocked to the area for the number of cheap visitor's *campements* or *gîtes* (around 17), built here for holiday makers.

They also came here because the **Basse Casamance National Park** offers a wealth of wildlife viewing and Cap Skirring on the south coast, is considered Senegal's most beautiful beach area. A ferry, which sails twice a week, links the regional capital to Dakar, the country's capital.

From The Gambia, the road through Brikama, south of Banjul, should be taken. It runs inland, crossing into Senegal after the frontier post at Jiboroh, at Seleti village. North of the wide Casamance estuary is a huge uninhabited swampland which the main road skirts as it runs south to **Ziguinchor**. This is the Casamance's main town, located up the Casamance estuary, in the south-east of the region. This small town lies about 100km (60 miles) south of The Gambia border.

Ziguinchor

The region's capital was founded by Portuguese traders in 1560 and is now a thriving market town. Veranda'd terraces of two-storey shops and houses line the wide, palm-lined boulevards, together with old French colonial buildings, and its large dock area moves a great deal of the agricultural produce of the region; fruit, vegetables, spices, palm products, cotton, rice, groundnuts and fish.

Souvenir hunters should look for the wonderful *Diola* sculptures produced here.

Palm Wine

Along West African roadsides you will see women selling fruit and other foods from makeshift stalls alongside which they also sell bottles corked with a screw of paper. These bottles contain either palm oil or palm wine. Palm oil is made from the fleshy part of the palm nut, or its fruit, and is deep yellow and like butter in its consistency. Palm oil is used in all West African cooking, lending it a particular flavour, and palm wine is for drinking! A blue-black local soap is also made from palm oil, as are candles.

Oil palm trees are tall and slender, bursting into leaf at the very top of the trunk. The palm fruit, a pillow-sized bunch of reddish palm nuts, grow down from the trunk under the fronds. The palm wine collector climbs the trunk by binding himself around it with a loop of rope, and edging up to just under the fronds where he punches a hole through the bark into the soft, sap-drenched wood. He inserts a tube made of leaves into the hole and fixes a bottle or gourd to the trunk, with the leaf funnel spout protruding into the container. He then leaves that tree and continues on to the next.

Returning after a few hours, the palm wine collector shins up the tree and finds that the sap has filled the bottle and the wine is ready to drink.

There are several varieties of this strong local drink. Newly tapped, palm wine is a sourish, white, frothy drink, best served chilled. Left for a short time, usually

just overnight, the wine quickly ferments and
becomes even more potent. Distilled, it is called
cana, and is so strong that it must be diluted with
syrup, when it is known as punch. Traditionally,
palm wine is drunk from a cup made from the seed
pod of the baobab tree, which is often called
monkey bread.

Above: Another bottle of potent palm wine being collected

Reservoir with a difference

Enampore is visited for its famous reservoir.

This rain water collection device was built in the form of a huge, thatched hut, double-roofed and forming a funnel which catches the rain and channels it into a central well. Inside, the hut is so large that it can house 50 people, including their cattle, goats and chickens. Locally, these reservoir huts are known as *case a impluvium*. The only other good example is that at Affiniam, due north, across the river from Ziguinchor, although there are several smaller ones in the Casamance area. You can stay overnight at either of these impluvium huts.

Ziguinchor makes a good jumping-off point from which to explore the huge Casamance region, but most visitors from The Gambia will not have sufficient time to see much of this area which has been likened to an African version of the Amazon estuary or the Carmargue. However, there are some very good hotels in Ziguinchor, from very cheap *campements* and guest houses to the luxurious Le Domaine de Nema-Kadior, or the Hotel Aubert.

Just outside Ziguinchor to the west, is the **Zoo and Botanical Gardens of Djibelor**, and a visit to **Bird Island**, a little way down the river, is another of the day or half-day excursions which can be made from the region's capital. A longer trip west, is the excursion to **Enampore**.

Sun-seekers head for the coast, particularly **Cap Skirring**, located almost on the border of Guinea-Bissau. It is a 70km (45 mile) drive west of Ziguinchor.

There are about 15 accommodations on this long, beautiful beach, ranging from *campement*-style inexpensive, basic lodging, to some quite high-class hotels. Cap Skirring is also a local village, much taken over by visitors. There are numerous excursions which can be taken from Cap Skirring. A visit up the coast to the much quieter beach and tiny village of **Diembereng** is a favourite, whilst inland, the fauna-rich National Park of Basse Casamance makes a fine day's outing.

The Niokolo-Koba National Park

Senegal's major national park is the **Niokolo-Koba**, located in the south east of the country, almost on the Guinea border. It is 550km (345 miles) from Dakar and is reached by either flying or taking the train to nearby Tambacounda from Dakar, or driving right up through The Gambia to Tambacounda and onward, the 80km (50 miles) to the park gates. **Simenti,** inside the park, also has a runway and accommodates charter plane services from Dakar.

A vast area of comparatively flat land 8,000km^2 (900,000 hectares) in area, it is open only during the dry season (December to June). The park is watered by the River Gambia which bisects it and its tributaries, the Niokolo-Koba and the River Koulountou. Most of the wildlife-spotting areas are around the waterways. There is both hotel and *campement* accommodation in and around the park, the most expensive of which is the beautifully located **Hotel de Simenti** in the village of the same name.

Further accommodation is located at the Dar Salam park entrance, at Badi, Bangane, Malapa, at Wouroli and Mako, on the southern border of the park and at Niokolo-Koba itself. Further south than the park's southern border, the Hippo Safari Lodge is almost on the Guinea border and the Campement du Lion is located near Simenti, near the centre of the park.

What will you see? As with most game parks, this depends on what animals and birds are around at the time you are there, how long you have to wait and watch for game, and how much you are prepared to travel within the park. The Niokolo-Koba is not like the great game parks of east and southern Africa, but it does contain a good number of mammals, 84 in all, around 350 species of bird life and many reptilian species.

This is the last refuge of Senegal's elephants, found generally near to Mount Assirik in the centre of the park and lions and leopards, found on the savannah tropical grasslands. The lion in Senegal are one of the largest varieties of lion in Africa. The rare giant derby (or western eland) is found here, as are waterbuck, bushbuck, roan antelope, buffalo, hartebeeste, bubale, guibe, chevrotan and kob.

In the rivers, crocodile, some up to 5m (16ft) in length, and hippo share the banks with river hogs and warthogs, and there are more than 60 different species of fish and aquatic reptiles in the park's waterways including the curious lungfish. Monitor lizards, some up to 2m (7ft) in length, come down to the water's edge where there are small turtles and terrapins.

Water snakes, python, mambas and puff adder are among the 30 snake varieties which inhabit the park, alongside the snake-eating mongoose and ant-eating pangolin and aardvark. In the high jungle galleries there are baboons, red, vervet, green, hussar and patas monkeys. There are also a few troupes of chimpanzee in the forest area. In the acacia-dotted grasslands there are gazelle, black antelope and duiker, stalked by striped and spotted hyena, jackal and wild dogs, under the constant gaze of lappet-faced vultures. Smaller mammals include the civet cat, serval, genet, crested and brush-tailed porcupine, and ground squirrel.

The varied vegetation of this park entices a great variety of bird life. The waterways and low grass-lands are home to African fin-foot, divers, crakes, kingfisher, stork, goose, duck, jacana, hammerkop, cormorant, heron, pelican, flamingo, ibis, egrets, crane, curlew and rail. Look for the woodpecker, shrike, widow bird, African emerald cuckoo, weaver, brown babbler, barbet, hoopoe, cordon blue, bee-eater, roller, sunbird, flycatcher, bunting, amethyst starling, fire finch, bulbul, wagtail, Senegal thick-knee, plover, pipit, lark, picapac, francolin, guineafowl, bustard, hornbill, violet turaco, lovebirds, African grey parrot and palm-nut vulture.

Raptor enthusiasts might see kestrel, scops owl, osprey, harrier, bateleur, goshawk and the Senegal coucal.

ACCOMMODATION

Ranging from the very basic to the luxurious, accommodation in The Gambia is varied and comparatively inexpensive. There are around 70 visitor hotels, guest houses,
country hotels and safari accommodations in the country.
Most visitors however will rarely use any other accommodation than the 20 or so custom-built beach hotels designed
for the tourist, apart from when on expeditions up-country.

Full details of all The Gambia's hotels can be obtained
from:
The Gambia Hotels Association
c/o The Bunbalow Beach Hotel
PO Box 2637, Serrekunda
The Gambia, West Africa.
☎ 465288, Fax: 466180.
www.gambiatourism.info

City Hotels

Few visitors to The Gambia opt for hotel accommodation in
Banjul itself, except the beach-side situated Atlantic hotel,
the country's first luxury hotel, opened in 1979. Most
visitors arrive on package holidays designed around the
beaches further south of the city.

Atlantic Hotel
Banjul, 408 rooms, 4 suites.
☎ 228601-6, Fax: 227861.

Carlton Hotel, Independence
Drive, Banjul, 90 beds.
☎ 228670. Fax: 227214.

Apollo Hotel, Orange Street,
Banjul, 90 beds. ☎ 228184.

Hotel Kantora
Independence Drive, Banjul.
90 beds. ☎ 228715.

Palm Grove, Mile 2, Banjul,
136 beds.
☎ 201620. Fax:201621

City Guest Houses

There are several city guest houses in Banjul, but most of
these cater for local travellers and the cost-conscious back-
packer. Among the best are the two listed here. One can
expect a certain degree of cleanliness, but very basic
accommodation in the city guest houses.

Abbey Guest House
Banjul, ☎ 225228.

Duma Guest House
Banjul, ☎ 228381.

Just out of town, at Cape St. Mary, on Afra Point, is the
Fawlty Towers bed and breakfast. ☎ 497653.

Beach Hotels

These hotels range from the luxurious, to the middle range
and inexpensive, mostly designed for beach-orientated
holidaymakers, many with pools and most with at least one
restaurant and an area of beach. However, some do not
have their own beaches but have access to a beach not far
from the hotel. Some are local hotels that have been
adapted to accommodate the foreign tourist.

The Laguna Beach Hotel
Denton Bridge, 672 rooms.
☎ 228236.

Cape Point Hotel
Cape St. Mary Bakau,
82 beds.
☎ 495005, Fax: 495375.

Mariatou Beach Hotel
Cape St. Mary Point,
400 rooms.
☎ 495143, Fax: 496484.

Sambou's Motel
Old Cape Road, Kololi,
20 rooms.
☎ 460630, Fax: 460023.

African Village
Bakau, 180 rooms.
☎ 495034, 495307,
Fax: 495307.

Friendship Hostel
Bakau, 148 rooms.
☎ 495830, Fax: 497344.

Fajara Hotel
Bakau, 600 rooms.
☎ 495605, Fax: 495531.

The Kombo Beach
Kotu Beach, 516 rooms,
8 suites.
☎ 465466-7, Fax: 465490.

Bungalow Beach
Kotu Beach, 224 rooms.
☎ 465288, Fax: 466180.

Kotu Strand Village Hotel
Kotu Beach, 90 rooms.
☎ 460950, Fax: 460954.

Safari Gardens Hotel
Fajara, 36 rooms.
☎ 495887, Fax: 496042.

Bakotu Hotel
Kotu Beach, 120 rooms.
☎ 465555.

Badala Park Hotel
Kotu Stream, 300 rooms,
20 suites.
☎ 460400, 460401,
Fax: 460402.

Palma Rima Hotel
Badala Parkway, 304 rooms.
☎ 463380-1, Fax: 463382.

Bantaba Hotel
Fajara Road, Kololi, 22 beds.
☎ 463767, Fax: 463767.

Bakadaji Hotel
Kotu Point, 48 beds.
☎ 462307.

Senegambia Beach Hotel
Kololi Beach, 650 rooms.
☎ 462717-9, Fax: 461839.

Banna Beach Hotel
150 rooms.
☎ 461177, Fax: 461255.

Kairaba Beach Hotel
P.M.B. 390, Serrekunda,
Kotu Beach, 294 rooms 3
suites.
☎ 462940-2, Fax: 462947.

Holiday Beach Hotel
Kololi, 90 beds.
☎ 460418, Fax: 460023.

Kololi Beach Club
Kololi. 100 rooms (timeshare
and self-catering villas).
☎ 463255, Fax: 464898.

Tafbel Maisonettes
Kololi, 48 beds.
☎ 460510, Fax: 460515.

Coconut Residence, Kololi,
1km, from beach. Colonial
style, 36 rooms.
☎ 463377?463399,
Fax: 461835.

Siva Sun Beach Hotel
Cape Point, Bakau,
450 rooms.
☎ 495428, Fax: 496102.

Beach Area Guest Houses

These hotels and guest houses are generally local
accommodations with basic standards, set inland from the
beach but not more than a short walk from the coast. They
range from the very small to the lower range
accommodations that just come up to tourist standards but
are inexpensive.

Fransisco's Guest House and Rooming Restaurant
Kairaba Avenue, Fajara,
8 rooms. ☎/Fax: 495332.

The Malawi. ☎ 393012.

YMCA Hostel. ☎ 392647.

Kololi Inn. ☎ 463410.

Keneba Hotel. 470093.

Bakadaji Hotel. ☎ 462307.

Kekoi's Happy Guest House
☎ 465544.

Mango Tree Guest House
☎ 460895.

Boucarabou
13 rooms. ☎ 812048-9.

There is also the small.
Luigi's Guest House.

Country Hotels

These are local hotels of an acceptable standard, expected of country accommodation, which are used by visitors looking for an overnight stay inland.

Lamin Lodge
Lamin, ☎ 495526.

Kemoto Hotel
☎ 990031, 990102.

Eddie's Hotel
Farafenni, ☎ 731259.

Fantasia Hotel, Farafenni.

Follonko Guest House
Kartong. VSO,
PO Box 677, Banjul.

Apollo 2 Hotel
Basse Santa Su.

Plaza Hotel
Basse Santa Su.

Lingure Hotel
Basse Santa Su.

Hotel Teranga
Basse Santa Su.

Gunjur Beach Motel
Gunjur, 8 beds.
☎ 486000, Fax: 486026.

Rest Houses

These accommodations are basic yet functional and generally clean enough for an overnight stay in areas where accommodation is scarce. Some are government rest houses where the key is kept at the local police station and can be pre-booked or available rooms can be taken on arrival.

Mansa Konko Rest House.

Ngala Lodge
Kololi, 20 rooms,
☎ 497672, Fax:497429.

Traveller's Lodge
Soma.

Georgetown Rest House
Georgetown.

Alakabung Lodge
Georgetown.

Traveller's Lodge
Bansang.

JEM Basse Rest House
Basse Santa Su, 10 beds.
☎ 668240/668356.

Agricultural Rest House,
Basse Santa Su.

Up-country Camps

Although the word safari is not used in The Gambia, lodges and camps are good bases for country treks. Most campsites are custom-designed for visiting tourists and up-country expeditions. Most also have all facilities like restaurant and

bar, running water and electricity. Some, however, are basic and designed for locals but are located in areas where there is no other accommodation.

Madiyana Bush Camp
Jinek, Paradise Island.
☎ 991994.

Kemoto Hotel
at Mootah Point, 100 beds.
☎ 460606, Fax: 460252.

Tendaba Camp
Tendaba, 130 beds.
☎ 406288, Fax: 466180.

Sofinyama Camp Site
☎ 49526.

Dreambird Camp
Georgetown, 12 beds.
☎ 676133.

Baobolong Camp
Georgetown.
☎ 676133.

The JangJang Bureh Campsite
Lamin Village,
Georgetown, 80 beds.
☎ 676182, or 495526 in Banjul.

Bird Safari Camp
Janjangbureh, 36 beds.
☎ 676108, Fax: 676120.

Gunjur Beach Motel
Gunjur, 8 beds.
☎/Fax: 486000.

Sanyang Nature Camp
Sanyang, 17 beds.
☎ 497186.

Jem Motel
Basse, 10 beds.
☎ 668356.

Sindola Safari Lodge
Kanilai, 80 beds.
☎ 483415.

Fuladu Camp
Basse, 36 beds.
☎ 668004.

Baobab Lodge
Kololi, 24 beds.
☎ 462170.

SENEGAL ACCOMMODATION

Since most visitors from The Gambia will only stay in either Dakar or at hotels pre-booked on organised excursions from The Gambia, the list of hotels available is not exhaustive. Hotel accommodation in central Dakar is rather more expensive than in The Gambia. Many cheap *campement* hotels exist throughout the country.

In the Sine-Saloum, near Missirah, there are the **Gîte de Bandiala** and the **Keur Saloum**, and others in the region at Toubacouta and Koalack, on the main Gambia to Dakar highway. **Ginak Island, or Paradise Island**, is located on the north border of the Gambia River, on the Senegalese border. It has African style accommodation for overnight stays. The three hotels in Niokolo Koba National Park are the: **Campement du Lion,** ☎ 321055, **Simenti Hotel,** ☎ 32804 and the **Badi**.

In Casamance there are many tourist resort hotels on Cap Skirring, including the **Club Mediterranee**, ☎ 935104, the **Hotel Savana**, ☎ 911552, **Hotel Kabrousse**, the **Royal Cap Hotel**, and the **La Paillote**, ☎ 935151.

CAR HIRE

For those staying at beachside hotels there is the opportunity to hire beach-buggies, mopeds or bicycles for used around the beach area and travelling up and down the coast. These are available from many of the beachside hotels. A valid International Driving Licence is needed. For up-country travel, unless you join one of the bush truck excursions or coach trips, you will need a four-wheel drive vehicle like a Land Rover, which can be hired from several agencies. They can be hired self-drive or with a driver.

Remember that there are very few garages in The Gambia and no breakdown services. There are around 3,220km (2,000 miles) of road throughout the Gambia, around 450km (280 miles) of which are paved or tarmaced. For a three-month period, an International Driving Licence is acceptable, and a UK driving licence can be used in the cases of short visits.

Car hire from:

Black and White Safaris Ltd
in Serekunda.
☎ 393174/393306.

Fransisco's
Atlantic Road.
☎ 495332.

Bacchus
Wadner Beach.
☎ 227948.

West African Tours
Bakau.
☎ 495258.

Gamtours
Kanifing, ☎ 392815.

The Gambia Experience
Kairaba Hotel.
☎ 460317.

Fact File

Hertz has an agency in the Senegambia at the Kairaba Hotels.

Avis is on Atlantic Avenue Bakau. ☎ 96119.

CHANGING MONEY, BANKS, CURRENCY AND CREDIT CARDS

The local money in The Gambia is the Dalasi, which is divided into 100 Bututs. Coins: 1, 5, 10, 25, 50 and 1 Dalasi; Notes: 5, 10, 25 and 50.

Senegal's currency is the CFA franc (100 CFA = 1 French franc). It is advisable to travel with French money in Senegal. There are numerous banks in Dakar, Senegal.

Money should be changed at the banks for the best rates. Hotels can change money, traveller's cheques etc. but charge extortionate exchange rates.

Commercial banks in The Gambia

Standard Chartered Bank (Gambia) Ltd
HQ – Banjul, branches: Westfield Junction, Fajara, Senegambia Hotel and Basse

Trust Bank
Branches: Banjul, Bakau, Westfield Junction, Brikama and Farafenni.

International Bank of Commerce
Branches in Bakau and Serrekunda.

Continent Bank
HQ: Kanifing, branches: Banjul and Brikama.

Arab-Ganbian Islamic Bank
Banjul.

Bank hours in Banjul
8am to 1.30pm Monday to Thursday.
8am to 11am Friday.

All banks elsewhere
8am to 12noon and 4.00pm Monday to Friday.
8am to 1pm Saturday.

ATM cash machines: these are available at Standard Chartered Bank in Banjul and branches in Fajara, Westfield Junction and Senegambia. Cardholdeers can withdraw money at any time.

Cheques: Standard Chartered Bank will also cash UK cheques of any amount. You will need to present your

passport for this service.

Euro cheques: euro cheques are also accepted but must be paid into an account.

Credit cards: most hotels and many restaurants within The Gambia accept Visa, MasterCard and American Express Cards. It is advisable to confirm with management before making a transaction.

Business Hours

Offices open from 8am to 4pm Monday to Thursday and 8 to 11am on Friday.

CLOTHING

A locally made Gambishirt, or a length of traditional batik, made into a *Kanga*, is the best solutions for light, comfortable beachwear. Although the climate is very hot during the day, the nights can grow cool and some shawl or light jacket is recommended for evenings. Head cover is essential in the strong sun, as are sunglasses. A raincoat, of the 'pacamac' variety, is advisable for sudden short showers if travelling in the wet season. Strong, comfortable walking shoes, or boots, are best for day-long sightseeing tours up-country. Sandals or flip-flops are ideal for the beach. Women should cover arms and the head, generally with a scarf, whilst visiting mosques and shoes should be removed. Bikinis should only be worn on the beach or within the confines of hotels.

CONSULATES

U.K. 48 Atlantic Road, Fajara. ☎ 495133, Fax: 496134.

U.S.A. Kairaba Avenue, Fajara. ☎ 391970, Fax: 492475.

Senegal. 10 Cameron Street. Banjul. ☎ 227469.

CRIME AND THEFT

There is very little crime in the country as punishment is summary and to be branded a thief or criminal in this Muslim country is tantamount to being banished from family and society in general.

Fact File

Tourist Police

In order to ensure total safety in the main resort areas the Government has set up a special police unit to serve the tourism development area. The headquarters is at Kotu Police Station and officers are often seen patrolling hotel areas. They are very friendly and are often seen chatting with tourists.

DOMESTIC AIR TRAVEL

The former Gambia Airways, or Gambia International Airways, is now known as Air Dabia. It operates one B747, and 3 or 4 smaller aircraft, flying to and from neighbouring countries

DRIVING IN THE GAMBIA

Apart from Banjul, where there are few road signs, bush driving rules predominate in the country. The town speed limit is 50kph (30mph).

Where possible, everybody drives on the right hand side of the road.

There are no laws regarding parking or seat belts. A valid International Driving Licence is required. Alcohol should be avoided when driving. The police are vigilant around the tourist areas. Always make sure you have sufficient fuel as it is not always available, especially up-country. Check your vehicle thoroughly when taking long distance drives. Check the weather when travelling on up-country roads as some parts can be impassable in the wet season. There are no breakdown services in The Gambia and engines tend to overheat easily in the heat. Report any accident directly to the nearest Police Station. Do not stop if you hit either a human or animal in the road, report it immediately. Never get out of the car to argue, to attempt to remove an obstacle or to check on any damage. Take sufficient drinking water with you always.

ELECTRICITY

As the Gambian national power supply can be erratic, most offices, hotels, restaurants and other public establishments have their own generators. The current is 220-230V. Battery operated travelling equipment, like shavers, is essential and a torch is always useful. Remember there is little or no street lighting. Senegal runs on the same voltage but the supply in the large towns is generally constant.

EMERGENCY TELEPHONE NUMBERS

Ambulance 16; Fire Service 18; Police 17, or 391970.

FACILITIES FOR THE DISABLED

There are few facilities for the disabled in The Gambia but as many tourist hotels are built bungalow-style there are few steps to negotiate, although there is always someone on hand to manhandle the wheelchair-bound disabled. Several hotels have made provisions for the invalid and your tour operator can advise on these.

HEALTH CARE

Before leaving home make sure you take all the medication you require for your stay abroad. The most common ailments for which visitors may require treatment are sun-burn and dehydration. Salt pills and quantities of non-alcoholic liquids diminish the effects of too much sun and calamine lotion is a useful addition to a first aid kit. It is sensible to pack an antiseptic like TCP in case of bites, stings or scratches and cuts from carelessly discarded containers left on the beach. A mild diarrhoeic may be a useful addition to the personal first aid pack if one is unused to spicy foods.

HEALTH HAZARDS

Pharmacies and General Practitioners at home now produce a compact health-care kit for travellers. As a precaution against accident, it may be wise to pack one of these kits. Dysentery, diarrhoea or other gastric problems, as in any other country, can be caught by eating badly prepared food or drinking contaminated water. Common sense should be used to avoid these problems. The likelihood of contracting Aids is a problem throughout West Africa and the relevant

Fact File

precautions should be taken. A good sun block lotion with the correct DEET content for the individual's complexion should be used. Nausea, lethargy, increased heartbeat, headaches and cramps are signs of sunstroke and medical treatment should be sought immediately should these symptoms occur. Sunglasses are a must in the African sun.

For a wasp or bee sting apply anti-histamine cream, and calamine lotion relieves insect bite irritation. Snakes rarely attack without provocation but should one get bitten, wipe the bite and cover with a cloth. Do not cut the bite. Apply a tourniquet above the bite if it is on a limb but do not cut off the blood supply. Try to identify the snake and seek medical attention immediately. Aspirin or alcohol, in moderation, eases the pain. Keep calm. A scorpion sting, not unusual in Africa, is best treated similarly to the bite of a snake - seek medical assistance directly. Confrontations with both snakes and scorpions are rare but are avoided by shaking out shoes etc. before dressing. Do not walk around barefoot and keep a watchful eye open in places where the creatures might lurk.

HOLIDAY INSURANCE

Visitors are advised to take comprehensive travel insurance covering the following: baggage, injury, death, illness, personal belongings, baggage damage/loss/delay.

INDEPENDENT TRAVEL

Independent travellers can feel safe to travel anywhere in The Gambia. The country is also nearly crime-free, as penalties for offenders are harsh. Up-country lodges and camp sites, plus the helpful attitude of the Gambians, have made independent travel in The Gambia a realistic and attractive option. Independent travelling in the country, provided the visitor realises that some accommodation can be most economical with facilities, cleanliness and services, can be a most rewarding way of seeing The Gambia. Prior booking of accommodation is recommended and this type of travel is by no means without its pitfalls; western-style organisation has still not reached The Gambia.

Fact File

LOCAL AND INTERNATIONAL DIALLING CODES

The international code for Banjul is (220). Local numbers begin with 2 in Banjul; 3 for Serekunda, and 4 for Bakau and Fajara. There are no regional code numbers for up-country except 6 for Base and 7 for Farafenni. These numbers should precede any old five-figure numbers. International calls can be made by dialling 000 first, followed by the code for the country. The Gamtel office is on Russell Street in Banjul.

LANGUAGE

English is the official language in The Gambia and French in Senegal. Local tribal languages include Mandinka (Mandingo). Wollof, Fula, Jola and Serahuli. Arabic is the third language as these are Islamic countries and lessons from the Koran (the Muslim Bible) are given in schools and mosques. French is the official language in Senegal, with many local African tribal languages.

LEFT LUGGAGE

Should you wish to travel up-country, or on an extended trip into Senegal, you can leave the luggage that you might not wish to take with you in any of the major hotels which have storage facilities.

LOST PROPERTY

Report this immediately to your tour guide, hotel manager or directly to the police.

MAPS

It is best to bring what maps you require with you. However, the Methodist Bookshop in Buckle Street, Banjul, has a small selection. ☎ 228179.

MOSQUITOES

Mosquitoes are the worst hazard of the Tropics, apart from the sun. Two million people a year die from malaria and

Fact File

this should be treated seriously. Anti-malarial pills should be commenced in advance of travelling abroad, and the course to be taken after returning should be rigorously adhered to. Consult your GP as to what anti-malarial treatment to take. If flu-like symptoms occur, even after returning home, a doctor should be consulted immediately. Perfume, after-shave and dark clothing attract mosquitoes and other insects. Mosquito repellent is useful, but not infallible. African mosquitoes operate at night and a mosquito net is the best deterrent. Keeping well covered after dark is wise.

MUSEUMS

There are few museums as such in The Gambia, the main national museum is in Banjul. It is open 8.00-16.00 Monday-Thursday and 8.00-13.00 Friday and Saturday.

NATIONAL TOURIST OFFICE

There is no Tourist Office as such in The Gambia, only the **Ministry of Information and Tourism** in New Admin Building, The Quadrangle, Banjul.

National Investment Promotion Authority, Independence Drive, Banjul. ☎ 228332, 228168, 229222, Fax: 229220.

NEWSPAPERS AND MAGAZINES

All newspapers and magazines are a rarity in The Gambia, although some hotels bring in a regular supply from abroad. Any reading matter is highly prized by the Gambians and it is a good idea to stock up with a few magazines to give away as gifts to the maid or houseboy. The Observer newspaper is now published three times a week in Bakau. There is a new paper available now:

The Point Newspaper
2 Garba Jahumpa Road
Bakau,
☎ 497441, Fax: 497442.

NIGHTLIFE

Most larger hotels organise their own entertainment like
African dancing, tribal performances, discos and folklore
musical sessions. The Oasis Nightclub in Banjul is the city's
liveliest place at night, open from 20.00-6.00am. At the
Atlantic Hotel on the city beach, there is the Dunda
Nightclub, ☎ 28601. On Cape Point there is Musu's Disco
and the Tropicana Nightclub on the way to the Senegambia
Hotel. Other beach hotels have nightclubs like the Bellengo
in the Kombo Beach Novotel, the nightclub in the
Senegambia Hotel, ☎ 92717. Hansen's Bar and the City
Disco in Serekunda double as nightclubs, as does the Safari
Club in Brikama. The African Village hotel in Bakau has a
European-style nightclub called Club 98 and there is live
night-time entertainment at the Tropicana Club in Kololi.
Two recently opened nightclubs are the Calabash with its
modern discotheques, playing a wide range of music from
calypso to Zouk and Wow and some UK and American
chart music, close to the Senegambia hotel, for Ndaga,
Zouk Jazz etc.

In Senegal there are numerous nightclubs and discos in
Dakar. Try the Sahel Club, Harry's Club, the Miami, or the
Kilimanjaro Club. There is a casino at Kololi in The Gambia
and one in Ngor, just outside Dakar, Senegal.

NUDISM

Topless sunbathing at the resort hotel poolside and on the
beach is not frowned on but common sense should be used
when walking around towns or public places. Wear shorts
or at least a *kanga*-type wrap when venturing outside the
hotel grounds or away from the beach. Nudism is not
permitted in The Gambia or Senegal.

PETS

It is not advisable to bring pets into The Gambia or Senegal.

PHARMACIES AND HOSPITALS

The Banjul Pharmacy is on Independence Avenue, Banjul. ☎ 227470, and at Wellington Street, Banjul. ☎ 227648. The Royal Victoria Hospital is located on Independence Drive, Banjul. ☎ 228223. Sweden Clinic: Dental Clinic and Laboratory, 8 Sait Maty Road, Bakau. ☎ 495934

The Medical Research Council is on Atlantic Road, Fajara. The private Westfield Clinic is in Serekunda. ☎ 292213. The Lamtoro Clinic is in Kololi. ☎ 460944. The only hospital outside Banjul is in Bansang, up-country.

PHOTOGRAPHY

The scenery in The Gambia is at times dramatic and often stunning. The coastal region offers some marvellous subjects for photography such as the fishing villages. As in any country, the photographing of airports and sensitive sites is forbidden and permission should be sought before photographing in museums and private homes. Photographs are one way to share holiday experiences of the country and its African charms. When taking a photograph first remember to load the film properly. Composition makes the difference between a good photograph and a snapshot. Frame the subject well, use trees, buildings, boats, and try different angles and unusual perspectives. Look for details in architecture, fishing boats, flowers etc. and get in close. Buy a few local postcards to show how a professional treats the scenic subjects and try to improve on these by varying the angles.

Try to include people, or activity in a photograph, it provides the focus even in photographs of comparatively uninteresting beaches or buildings, although you will be hard pushed to find an uninteresting scene in The Gambia. Always ask permission before taking a photograph of someone you do not know. Lighting conditions make it an excellent location for good, clear photographs during the day although early morning and late afternoon are best to avoid strong light. Don not forget that sunrise, sunset, and even moonlight, can produce unusual and effective results. The intense reflection off white sandy beaches and the surface of water like the river and the sea, can ruin a good photograph. A skylight filter is useful, not only in cutting out glare, but to protect the lens. Photographic experimentation and ingenuity make those memories even more rewarding. Take sufficient film with you although most types of film can be bought in hotel shops, but check expiry dates. Processing film locally is quite expensive.

POSTAL SERVICES

The post in The Gambia is good and cheap and most hotels have postboxes. The main Post Office is on Russell Street in Banjul. Stamps are available at most hotels

PUBLIC HOLIDAYS AND FESTIVALS

The Gambia and Senegal observe the religious holidays of both Christianity and Islam and these include Christmas, Ramadan which lasts for thirty days, and other Islamic celebrations like Tobaski and Koriteh, calculated by the phases of the moon. Check the current Muslim calendar dates before you travel. It is unwise to eat or drink in public during the day whilst the fasting period of Ramadan is being observed. Do not enter mosques during prayer time if you are not Muslim. Political holidays like Independence Days are also national holidays.

New Years Day is observed; February 18th is Gambian Independence Day; Good Friday and Easter Monday are public holidays, as is May Day. August 15th is Assumption Day and Christmas Day is also a holiday. April 4th and June 20th are both Independence Days in Senegal.

CULTURAL EVENTS

So diverse are the tribes and sub-divisions of tribes in Sene-gambia that a book could be dedicated to the numerous tribal celebrations, observances and society rituals which occur throughout the year. These might include initiation ceremonies, harvest festivals, ritual battles, rain dances, purification dances, fertility dances, and spirit appeasement festivals.

Around Christmas and New Year, the celebrations of the *Fanals* can be watched in both The Gambia and in Senegal.

Fact File

These are the procession of split bamboo and paper decorative lanterns, often connected to the fishing business, where lanterns are made in the shape of fishing boats. Clubs or teams parade their boats in a competition much like a carnival procession. The parades are accompanied by bands with trumpets and drummers. See examples of the *fanals* in the museum in Banjul, or in Dakar's museums.

The International Roots Festival, connected with the Homecoming of the African Diaspora, and featuring a carnival, traditional sporting events, dances, music, arts and craft exhibitions and trade fairs, history tours and fashion shows, has been celebrated annually, generally during June, since 1987.

In Dakar and St Louis, Senegal, *pirogue* races, in canoes manned by around 30 paddlers, are held around Christmas time. Celebrations relating to the farmers' sale of groundnuts occur during December and January

PUBLIC TOILETS

There are few public toilets anywhere in the country. In Banjul it is suggested that one uses the toilet in the African Heritage restaurant on Wellington Street. In Serekunda there is one at the bush taxi depot and also in the Abuko Nature Reserve.

PUBLIC TRANSPORT

Buses

The Gambia Public Transport Corporation operate blue buses which run inexpensive services around the Banjul, Bakau and Serekunda areas, and ply express routes up country to Basse Santa Su (10 hours) and Fatoto, and a regular route twice a day between Banjul and Dakar (5 hours). The non-express routes can take much longer and make many stops on the journeys.

There is no train service in the country, but a bus service operates for up-country travel, and can be taken from the depot in Kanafing.

Taxis

Taxi fares should always be negotiated in advance, even though rates are usually displayed on notice boards. Tourist taxis, painted green with a diamond sign and a serial number on the side, are authorised by the Tourist Board, which should be contacted in cases of queries. These are dedicated to tourists. Yellow and green town taxis are mainly four-passenger saloon cars that run a shared service over short distances or park by the roadside for individual hire.

Apart from the inexpensive, yellow number plate tourist taxis and green and yellow town taxis, which ply the residential and hotel routes with the availability of day hire for longer excursions, the bush (collective) taxis are the predominant means of local long-haul transport. Bush taxis, or *taxis-brousse* in Senegal, cover the entire country and are a cheap, but uncomfortable way of getting around. These are mainly seven-passenger saloon cars, vans and minibuses. They do not have a single colour and they operate a shared service over both short and long distances. They have a set fare. It is advisable to ask the fare before boarding the vehicle. One downside is that they can be very slow as they tend to make several stops on the way to allow passengers to board or disembark. Serekunda bush taxi park is the centre from which most bush taxis ply their routes up-country.

Boats

A regular tourist boat service plies the river from Lamin Lodge to Georgetown. This makes several stops en-route with two overnight stops, taking three days to cover the distance. Departure is on Wednesday morning and arrival in Georgetown is late Friday evening. The return river trip takes two days, leaving Georgetown on Saturday morning and arriving at Lamin Lodge on Sunday. Accommodation can be on board (no cabins) or at the campsites at the stopovers. On board are bar, toilet and sun-deck, with a basic galley for meals. Contact: Gambia River Excursion, PO Box 664, Banjul. ☎ 495526.

If you are in The Gambia during the groundnut harvest, December-January, you may find a helpful groundnut barge

captain who would negotiate a river trip on his traditional craft.

Ferries

Ferries between Banjul-Barra-Banjul, run every two hours, a crossing of 20-40 minutes. 8.00-18.00 Daily.

Farafenni-Mansa Kongo (Transgambia Highway route). No set times, often a long wait.

North Bank-MacCarthy Island (Georgetown)-South Bank. No set times, no charge.

RADIO

The Government Radio Gambia broadcasts in English and local languages. The Swedish-operated Radio Syd broadcasts European and African music, news in English and Swedish, and local information. Radio Senegal broadcasts in French and local language and Senegalese television programmes can be received in The Gambia.

SHOPPING

Apart from the fixed prices of goods in shops, supermarkets and at hotels, few other goods on sale have a set price! Haggling is time-consuming but is the only way to make sensible purchases. Start at around one-third of the asking price. Good bargains can be had in the markets for batik, tie-dye and local print, or Lagos cloth. Clothes are inexpensive and can be run up in any design or pattern. Gambishirts, gold and silver filigree jewellery, carved wooden objects, dolls in traditional dress and beads, are all a popular buy. Near many resort hotels, there are *Bengdulalu*, or African type market stalls, with a variety of handicraft on sale. Remember not to buy artefacts made from prohibited animal products.

Brikama Craft Market
☎ 484654.

Dam.S.S.Sallah Craft (Wood) Store
28 Bakau Cape Point, Bakau, ☎370075/496469.

Kanbeng Lessirila Kaffo Craft and Musical Instruments
Inyambia Gighway, opposite Brikama Police Station.

SUPERMARKETS

There are well-stocked supermarkets in Banjul, Bakau and Serrekunda and along the mixed business and residential area of Kairaba Avenue. The main supermarkets are: St Mary's, Harry's, Maroun's GSC, Atson's Kairaba, Happiness Stop Step and Shop, Sony's and A-Z.

SPORTS AND PASTIMES

Wrestling is the national sport in Senegambia and football is becoming very popular. Cricket matches are sometimes held on the Quadrangle Square in Banjul. Wrestling matches can be seen in most large towns on Saturday and Sunday evenings, except during the Muslim festival of Ramadan.

Golf

There is an 18-hole course at the Fajara Club with nine par 4, seven par 3, and two par 5 holes. Temporary membership is available.

Watersports

Windsurfing, surfboarding, small dinghy sailing and other watersports are available at most large beach-side hotels, but, as there are few reefs here, diving and scuba diving is limited to the estuaries but is not recommended. There is a diving club in Dakar, Senegal.

Walking

The climate and distances do not make for good walking excursions except in wildlife reserves like Abuko and on birdwatching trips.

Fishing

The very nature of the Senegambia, being based largely on the fishing industry around the rivers, *bolongs*, waterways, deltas, estuaries and the coast, means that the fisherman is in his element. Fishing from the beach or riverbank is easy, but a *pirogue* can be hired specially for fishing trips just about anywhere. Organised fishing excursions can be booked through most of the larger hotels and through LA

Creek Fishing, ☎ 991313, or Il Monda, ☎ 466573. Both offer either delta, *bolong*, river, or deep-sea game fishing trips. In Senegal there are sports fishing clubs in Dakar, the Saloum delta and Casamance.

Birdwatching

Even if you have no interest in ornithology, you will, at one time or another in Senegambia, be enthralled by the region's striking and colourful bird life. Organised bird-watching tours contact: West African Tours, ☎ 495258, Gamtours, ☎ 392359, Five-Star Tours, ☎ 371110, or through most of the larger hotels.

Racket sports/snooker

Tennis, volleyball, basketball, squash, badminton and snooker are available at most large tourist hotels, but try the Reform Club in Banjul and the Cedars Club in Serekunda for good tennis.

TELEPHONE SERVICES

Gamtel, the national telecommunications service is good and telephone, telex, telegram and fax services are all available in Banjul, Bakau, Serekunda and most large hotels. There are lots of tele centres now around the resort areas. For your own convenience you can also buy an international phone card from Gamtel. The Gambia is also catching up rapidly with the latest technology in commun-ication, hence the presence of Internet cafés in both Banjul and Kairaba.

Cyber cafés

Quantum Net Co Ltd
– the main Internet service provider in The Gambia.

**Midway Centre
Kairaba Avenue Café**
☎396600.

**Bakau New Town and
Kairaba Avenue Junction
Cafés**, ☎ 494514.

Westfield Cafés
☎ 393500.

Banjul Cafés
☎ 202627.

Bakau Café
☎ 494382.

Senegambia Café
☎ 460739.

TIME

The Gambia and Senegal are on Greenwich Mean Time throughout the year, and 5 hours ahead of New York time.

TIPPING

Tipping is not obligatory in The Gambia as a service charge is generally added to hotel and restaurant bills. However, porters, hotel staff, taxi drivers and guides do expect a small gratuity.

WATER

The water in The Gambia is usually potable but one can always purchase noted brands of bottled water, particularly in the shops and supermarkets of holiday resort areas.

HOLIDAY READING

Apart from a couple of guidebooks, one of which the author of this book wrote, there is very little literature available on The Gambia, and even less on Senegal in English.

The most famous book relating to The Gambia and its history of slave-trading, is the novel *Roots*, by the American author, Alex Haley. In this he traces his ancestry back to the banks of the Gambia River at Juffure. For wildlife enthusiasts there is *A Naturalist's Guide to The Gambia* by Etienne Edberg, published in Sweden. History buffs will be intrigued by the explorer, Mungo Park's account of his journeys in The Gambia and beyond, in *Travels into the Interior of Africa*, or J. M. Gray's 1966 *History of The Gambia*. Historians and those interested in politics might want to read *Political History of The Gambia 1816-1994*, by Arnold Hughes and David Perfect. Anthropologists will be interested to read *Ethnic Groups of the Senegambia*, by Patience Sonko-Goodwin. There are several poetry books available by local Gambian poets. The Rough Guide to World Music has a large section on West African music and there are general books on African art and culture like *African Traditional Architecture*, *African Art*, *African Textiles* and even *African Hairstyles*.

Index

Published by
Landmark Publishing Ltd,
Ashbourne Hall, Cokayne Ave, Ashbourne
Derbyshire DE6 1EJ England

2nd Edition
ISBN 1-84306-077-9
© **Andy Gravette 2003**

British Library Cataloguing in Publication Data: a catalogue record for this
book is available from the British Library.

Print: Gutenburg Press Ltd, Malta
Editor: Kay Coulson
Cartography: James Allsopp
Design: Samantha Witham

Cover Pictures
Front: Coos flour is still pounded by traditional methods
Back: Both the Atlantic Ocean and Gambia River offer
excellent fishing opportunities

Picture Credits:
Andy Gravette: Front cover, 23M, 31b, 31c, 31e, 35all, 47M, 47B,
54TL, 54TR, 59M, 59B, 67BL, 67BR, 82M, 82BR, 86, 87, 91, 94all,
102M, 102B, 103, 106all, 115all, 123
Ashley Ashworth: 15, 59T, 75
Gambia Hotel Association: Back cover, 23B, 26, 31a, 31d,
39, 67T, 67M, 82BL, 114, 126all
John Peck: 47T, 54B, 82T
Photobank: 3, 6/7, 23T, 42, 63, 71, 79, 99, 110, 131
Julie Meech: 19all
Gambia Tourist Board: 102T